CHRISTIANS AND ROMAN RULE
IN THE NEW TESTAMENT

COMPANIONS TO THE NEW TESTAMENT

CHRISTIANS AND ROMAN RULE IN THE NEW TESTAMENT

New Perspectives

RICHARD J. CASSIDY

A Herder and Herder Book
The Crossroad Publishing Company
New York

The Crossroad Publishing Company
481 Eighth Avenue, New York, NY 10001

Printed in the United States of America

Library of Congress Cataloging-in-Publication Data

Cassidy, Richard J.
    Christians and Roman rule in the New Testament : new perspectives / Richard J. Cassidy.
        p.   cm.
    "A Herder and Herder book."
    Includes bibliographical references and index.
    ISBN 0-8245-1903-5 (alk. paper)
    1. Bible. N.T.—Criticism, interpretation, etc.   2. Rome in the Bible.   I. Title.
    BS2545.R65 C37 2001
    225.9'5—dc21
                                                            2001000505

1   2   3   4   5   6   7   8   9   10   04   03   02   01

DEDICATION

For Fred and Sue Lawrence, L. Glenn and Jane O'Kray, and
their respective families; for the St. Hugo Justice and
Peace families; for Dean Brackley, S.J., in El Salvador;
and once again for the members of the extended
Detroit Catholic Worker (Day House) community.

Contents

Preface to the Series, by Charles Talbert   ix

Preface   xi

Chapter One
Christians and Roman Rule:
Overview and Methodology   1

Chapter Two
Characteristic Features of Roman Imperial Rule
during the New Testament Era   5

Chapter Three
Jesus and Roman Rule in the Synoptic Gospels   19

Chapter Four
John's Gospel and Roman Power   37

Chapter Five
The Acts of the Apostles and Roman Rule   51

Chapter Six
The Perspective of Paul in Romans
and the Perspective of 1 Peter   68

Chapter Seven
The Perspective of Paul in Chains   84

Chapter Eight
Revelation and the Destruction of Roman Power   104

Chapter Nine
Overview of Christians and Roman Power
in the New Testament Writings   125

Bibliography   136

Index of Ancient Sources   140

Index of Names and Subjects   143

Maps

The Roman World in the Early First Century   4

The Locations of Early Christian Communities
     under Roman Rule   124

Preface to the Series

THE COMPANIONS TO THE NEW TESTAMENT SERIES aims to unite New Testament study with theological concerns in a clear and concise manner. Each volume:

- engages the New Testament text directly.
- focuses on the religious (theological/ethical) content of the New Testament
- is written out of respect for the integrity of the religious tradition being studied. This means that the New Testament is studied in terms of its own time and place. It is allowed to speak in its own terms, out of its own assumptions, espousing its own values.
- involves cutting-edge research, bringing the results of scholarly discussions to the general reader
- provides resources for the reader who wishes to enter more deeply into the scholarly discussion.

The contributors to the series are established scholars who have studied and taught the New Testament for many years and who can now reap a wide-ranging harvest from the fruits of their labors. Multiple theological perspectives and denominational identities are represented. Each author is free to address the issues from his or her own social and religious location, within the parameters set for the series.

It is our hope that these small volumes will make some contribution to the recovery of the vision of the New Testament world for our time.

Charles H. Talbert
Baylor University

Preface

TWENTY-FIVE YEARS AGO in Berkeley, California, I experienced a fully unanticipated outpouring of grace that led eventually to the formal publication of an analysis of Luke's Gospel. In various academic and pastoral settings, the journey that began with Luke's Gospel continued with studies on the Acts of the Apostles, the Gospel of John, and the Letters of Paul. The present study stands in direct continuity with these previous works and, in effect, consolidates their principal insights. I thus begin by expressing my profound gratitude to Luke, John, and Paul, and the other sacred authors whose writings I have been privileged to interpret.

In his approach to the process of knowing, Bernard Lonergan, S.J., consistently emphasized the importance of the questions with which a person begins his or her investigations. This insight of Fr. Lonergan's has been confirmed in my own efforts to interpret the texts of the New Testament writers. Because of my own initial experiences in social ministry and because of my presence in courtroom settings where Catholic Worker friends have eloquently spoken of their allegiance to the risen Jesus, I have been impelled to consider the political counsel of the New Testament afresh and to ask new questions of certain key passages. I thus wish to express my gratitude once again for the witness of many exemplary friends during the early stages of my ministerial and academic journeys. Their lives of radical allegiance have been a grace unto me in multifaceted ways.

Regarding the publication of this book, I am distinctly conscious of a writing dimension and a publishing dimension. With respect to the writing dimension, a Lonergan Fellowship at Boston College in the Spring semester of 2000 provided the precise window of opportunity that was needed to complete this manuscript. I am grateful to Professor Fred Lawrence and Fr. Joseph Flanagan, S.J., for their roles in the awarding of this Fellowship. I am also grateful to Cardinal Adam Maida, of the Detroit Archdiocese, and to Cardinal Bernard Law, of the Boston Archdiocese, for their kind efforts in arranging for me to reside at St. John's Seminary in Brighton for the duration of the sabbatical.

At St. John's, Msgr. Richard Lennon, Fr. Arthur Coyle, the faculty, seminarians, and staff members were all so warmly welcoming that I felt I was experiencing something of the rapport that Paul felt with the Christian community at Philippi. A comparable cordiality was also expressed to me by the professors, fellows, and staff members at the Lonergan Center and by the members of the New Testament Colloquium of the Boston Theological Institute. Because Professor Edward Hobbs, originally the director of my doctoral dissertation at Berkeley, is actively engaged in this Colloquium, its meetings were especially stimulating and pleasurable for me. Similarly, it was a pleasure for me to renew friendship with Fr. William Neenan, S.J., once my mentor in Economics at the University of Michigan and now serving as University Vice-President at Boston College.

The friendship dimension of being on sabbatical was also experienced through frequent suppers with Fred and Sue Lawrence, whose faithfulness I have cherished for thirty years. This dimension was again expressed through the arrival of a group of family members and friends for the festive weekend of April 17th. I am grateful to Sharon Cassidy Snider, Glenn O'Kray, Joan Wagner, S.S.J., Margaret Golden, V.S.C., Margaret Gardner, and to Elizabeth and Matthew Wawro and their family for their participation in the endeavors and celebrations of that weekend.

With respect to the elements pertaining to the publication of the book, it is only appropriate to begin with mention of the roles played by Professor Charles Talbert, the General Editor of this series and the President of the Catholic Biblical Association for

1999–2000. Charles proposed this volume to me just as I was completing my manuscript treating Paul's prison writings. He, his wife, Betty (who serves as Director of Spiritual Formation at Truett Seminary of Baylor University), and I had come to know each other well from the annual meetings of the Catholic Biblical Association. However, at the time of Charles's invitation, we had no way of knowing that the year of our closest collaboration would also be the interval in which our three dear fathers would depart this life. There was, then, in the interweaving of our lives and our scholarship a particular poignancy, one that all three of us came to treasure deeply. Professor Barbara Green, O.P., also entered into collaboration at this time, according a thorough review to my completed manuscript and providing many helpful suggestions relative to clarity and readability.

Because of my relative unfamiliarity with word processing (her recent retirement also meant that Rose Marie Beale's dedicated secretarial assistance was no longer available to me), I have turned to various seminarians and staff members at Christ the King Seminary for assistance in making the corrections and adjustments that are inevitable in the last stages prior to the publication. Michael Tubridy, Lynn Shumway, and Lynn Morgan all contributed estimably to the process at this stage. In addition, I have benefited from the steps taken to support this book by Fr. Richard Siepka, CKS Rector, and by Patrick Hulsman, Alan Meister, Diana Damstetter, and Patricia Neuman of the Seminary's Office for Institutional Advancement. Their efforts represented a continuation of the support for my research and writing that I have been pleased to receive here at Christ the King. I also wish to acknowledge the careful arrangements relative to the scholarly presentation of this book that were achieved by Dr. Maurya Horgan and Dr. Paul Kobelski of The HK Scriptorium.

Throughout the entire process of transforming a manuscript into a book, it has proved extremely satisfying to work with Gwendolin Herder, Alison Donohue, and Michael Parker at Crossroad/ Herder and Herder. For Charles and Betty Talbert and myself, the Society of Biblical Literature Annual Meeting in Nashville in November of 2000 was an occasion for interacting and celebrating memorably with these and other members of the Crossroad staff.

The return of the Herder and Herder imprint to prominence in U.S. publishing is indeed a development to be welcomed. May the publication of this book carry forward the work of reverence-filled presentation and interpretation that was originally embarked upon by such as Matthew, Mark, Luke, John, and Paul. May the publication of this book provide a significant new resource for every Christian striving to discern her or his path of discipleship within the contemporary contexts for social and political life.

1

Christians and Roman Rule
Overview and Methodology

A T THE OUTSET OF THIS STUDY analyzing the topic of Christians and Roman rule in the New Testament, it is useful to highlight the following teaching of Jesus:

> A dispute arose among them, which of them was to be regarded as the greatest. And he said to them, "The kings of the Gentiles exercise lordship over them; and those in authority over them are called benefactors. But not so with you; rather let the greatest among you become as the youngest, and the leader as one who serves. For which is the greater, one who sits at table, or one who serves? Is it not the one who sits at table? But I am among you as one who serves" (Luke 22:24–27; cf. Mark 10:41–45; Matt. 20:24–28).

As this study unfolds and presents a wide-ranging analysis of the New Testament writings, the above passage will exercise a lapidary influence. At this point it is premature to enter into a detailed exegesis of these verses. Nevertheless, on the lips of Jesus, references to "rulers of the Gentiles" and "benefactors" bespeak a familiarity with the patterns of the surrounding Roman empire. Moreover, it was not only during the ministry of Jesus that the Roman authorities were dominant. The empire administered by these authorities provided a political context for every first-century Christian as well as for every New Testament text by and about these disciples.

Because it is desirable to consider the characteristics of the Roman rule that these Christians faced, chapter 2 of this study will present a brief analysis of the objectives and patterns of the Roman authorities during the first Christian century. The remainder of this book will then analyze the responses to Roman power given by Jesus and by his disciples as these responses are described within the Gospels, the Acts of the Apostles, the Pauline letters, 1 Peter, and Revelation.

In utilizing Luke's Gospel and the Acts of the Apostles, considerations regarding the evangelist's personal perspective on Roman rule are significant. Luke provides a range of descriptions concerning the responses given by Jesus and his disciples, but what perspective did Luke himself have relative to Roman rule? A similar question will be posed regarding the perspective of the final author of the Gospel of John.

When it comes to determining Paul's perspective on the Roman system, further methodological issues emerge. First, there is the matter of the tension between Luke's portrait of Paul in the Acts of the Apostles and the portrait of Paul that emerges from any analysis of his own letters. Second, there is the striking divergence among interpreters of Paul's writings over whether such letters as Colossians, Ephesians, and 2 Timothy are authentically from Paul's own hand. Third, there is the intriguing question of whether Paul's perspective changed over time. Clearly the resolution of this last question will involve judgments about the sequence in which Paul's undisputed letters were written.

In general, the present study is *canonical* in the sense that its principal focus is the New Testament documents as finished works included within the canon of the New Testament. This is in distinction to a more source-oriented approach that seeks to establish the sources utilized for each document and, especially regarding the Gospels, strives to determine the nature of the document at earlier stages of composition. The approach of this study is also distinct from the approach of those commentaries on the New Testament writings that assign a probable date of composition for each document. Chapter 7 below will argue tenaciously that Philippians was written after Romans and after Philemon. Nevertheless, throughout the remainder of this study, indeterminacy will be a rule of thumb regarding the final dates of each of the Gospels and for the Acts of the Apostles, 1 Peter, and Revelation.

Bearing these methodological considerations in mind, it is now appropriate to proceed to chapter 2 and an examination of the Roman milieu in which all of the documents that will be analyzed in this study were composed. Chapters 3 through 8 will then provide an in-depth analysis of these documents. Finally, chapter 9 will explicate the relevance of these first-century writings for biblically oriented Christians in the third millennium.

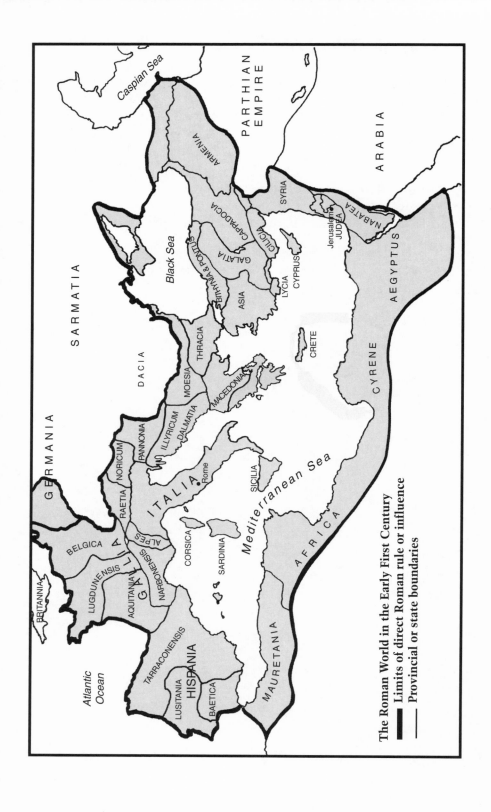

The Roman World in the Early First Century

▬ Limits of direct Roman rule or influence

— Provincial or state boundaries

BRITANNIA

GERMANIA

SARMATIA

Caspian Sea

PARTHIAN EMPIRE

ARMENIA

ARABIA

Black Sea

CAPPADOCIA

SYRIA

CILICIA

NABATEA

Jerusalem
JUDEA

GALATIA

BITHYNIA & PONTUS

CYPRUS

AEGYPTUS

DACIA

ASIA

LYCIA

THRACIA

CRETE

CYRENE

MOESIA

MACEDONIA

ILLYRICUM

DALMATIA

PANNONIA

NORICUM

RAETIA

ITALIA

Rome

SICILIA

Mediterranean Sea

AFRICA

ALPES

BELGICA

GALLIA

LUGDUNENSIS

AQUITANIA

NARBONENSIS

CORSICA

SARDINIA

MAURETANIA

Atlantic Ocean

TARRACONENSIS

LUSITANIA

HISPANIA

BAETICA

2

Characteristic Features of Roman Imperial Rule during the New Testament Era

T O DESCRIBE THE COMPLEX REALITY of Roman rule during the first Christian century is more a task for an encyclopedia than for a single chapter. What follows is thus only a sketch of certain fundamental features. In its essential lines, this presentation draws upon the analyses of Roman rule that I have previously made in works treating the Gospel of Luke, the Gospel of John, the Acts of the Apostles, and the letters of Paul.[1] This presentation is divided into three parts. The first and longest section sketches the character of the imperial system that Augustus evolved. The next section focuses on Augustus' successors, especially Nero, as they themselves functioned as overseers of this vast system. The final section very briefly considers two paradigmatic responses by those subjugated under Roman rule.

ROMAN RULE
WITH REFERENCE TO AUGUSTUS

Because Augustus was the principal architect of the Roman imperial system, his reign (31 B.C.–A.D. 14) is critically significant for an understanding of the Roman empire and for an understanding of the functioning of the Christian movement within that system. Nevertheless, several key factors of Roman practice were well

5

established prior to Augustus. For example, Roman expansion through violent conquest long antedated Augustus, and Roman leaders prior to Augustus had evolved mechanisms for the economic exploitation of the peoples they subjugated. The practice of consigning large segments of the subjugated populations to slavery was among these mechanisms. At the end of the Republic, slaves may have accounted for 25 percent of the population of Italy proper. The percentage varied throughout the provinces, but note that slavery, strictly speaking, was not practiced in the Jewish society of Palestine.[2]

Roman commanders prior to Augustus were certainly motivated by the status and glory they derived from exercising military power. Nevertheless it was Augustus who first received the supreme glory of ruling a unified empire. Prior to Augustus, Roman leaders had assimilated the Italian peninsula and then subsequently extended Roman rule to Sicily, Sardinia, parts of Spain and Africa, territories in the Aegean peninsula and in Asia Minor, and territories in the northwest. Augustus himself initiated a comprehensive campaign in Spain and oversaw significant new conquests in the Alpine region and in the Balkan territories. Indeed, the incorporations accomplished during his reign virtually doubled the size of the empire. At his death the total population of the imperial territories may have been fifty-four million with approximately eight million residing in Italy and approximately one million in Rome itself.

Augustus came to full power as a result of a complex series of political and military conflicts. After the assassination of Julius Caesar by Cassius and Brutus (senators who bitterly resented Caesar's usurpations of dictatorial power), Octavian, Caesar's heir, had formed an alliance with Mark Antony and Lepidus and had vanquished the assassins and their forces. Civil war subsequently ensued between the forces of Octavian and those of Mark Antony and Cleopatra. Octavian prevailed at the Battle of Actium in 31 B.C. and acceded to power as *princeps,* an office that enabled him to exercise sovereign authority in cooperation with the Roman senate. Always sensitive to the sympathies of senators who desired a restoration of the Republic, Octavian refrained from explicitly claiming the powers and perquisites of a dictator. He did, however, accept the honorific "Augustus" and was frequently referred to by that title as if it were his proper name.

Augustus' astuteness in presenting his rule as similar to that of a constitutional monarch enabled him to consolidate a vast amount of power in his own hands without engendering serious resistance from the Roman senate. Augustus displayed ingenuity in allocating the plunder, the slaves, and the revenues that the Romans derived from their subjugated territories. He instinctively grasped that, if he himself were going to survive and prosper in his chosen role as princeps, he would have to provide well for (a) the senatorial and equestrian classes, (b) the populace of Rome, and (c) the soldiers who made up Rome's various military forces.

In considering the mechanisms the Romans used to distribute the goods and revenues that they extracted from the provinces, it should first be noted that Augustus and his successors all became prodigiously wealthy individuals. In addition to a vast personal treasury, Augustus came to hold extensive properties in various parts of the empire and acquired an enormous number of slaves. To varying degrees, the prominent members of the senatorial and equestrian classes also shared in these forms of wealth. In addition, these groups benefited from sharing in the extensive trade that flourished within the boundaries of the empire on terms that were highly favorable to those well positioned in Rome.

Augustus' policy of free grain distribution was intended to confer a significant benefit upon those members of the populace of Rome who were eligible for this monthly dole. The logistics and the expense of assuring the regular availability of such a huge amount of corn were indeed formidable challenges. Nevertheless, maintaining the loyalty of the masses in Rome to the reigning emperor was critical. The regularly held games and spectacles considered in tandem with the monthly grain dole show that there is considerable truth in the common understanding of "bread and circuses." Through this strategy, Augustus and the various Roman emperors after him strove to maintain their rapport with the populace of Rome.

Also critical to Augustus' longevity in office was the spectacular support that he received from the various components of the Roman military: the praetorian guard, the legionaries, and the auxiliaries. Rome's standing armies were vast. At the end of Augustus' reign, as many as twenty-five legions were in existence with an approximate total of 125,000 legionaries. Since auxiliary troops drawn from the provinces were increasingly used to complement the legions, 300,000 or more soldiers served the Roman cause during the middle years of the first century. In addition, nine elite cohorts, the praetorian guard, provided personal security to the emperor and the members of the imperial family.

How was the loyalty of the Roman military secured? An annual salary, donatives, and a substantive discharge payment were essential elements in the military's compensation. In addition, citizenship was granted to those serving in the legions; these legionaries also received a significant grant of land upon the completion of twenty-five years service. In the case of the auxiliaries, the completion of twenty-five years of service brought with it the reward of Roman citizenship.

Augustus' arrangements for his military merit further consideration because of the multiple objectives they achieved. The soldiers' morale and the loyalty of the army as a whole were perhaps the most evident and important benefits. However, another set of benefits came from the practice of awarding the land grants in such a way that discharged soldiers were grouped into "colonies," settlements that were positioned at strategic locations within the boundaries of the empire. These concentrations of Roman citizen-veterans promoted the stability and loyalty of a given province and also served as a deterrent to external aggressors.[3]

Clearly, a steady, predictable flow of revenue and resources toward Rome was essential if Augustus' programs for benefiting the Roman upper classes (including Augustus himself), the populace of Rome, and the Roman military were to be sustained over time. Roman leaders prior to Augustus had imposed taxation upon the peoples they subjugated. To finance the administration of what had now become a vast empire, Augustus and his successors reorganized, expanded, and centralized Roman taxation.

Within the system that Augustus evolved, there was considerable variety in the arrangements under which particular provinces and subjugated territories were administered and taxed. However, regardless of the exact mechanism for collecting taxes in a given province or territory, *maximum* tax revenues always remained the imperial objective. Further, there was no lack of imagination regarding the types of taxes that could be employed!

The surviving records indicate that the Roman authorities collected the following taxes within the province of Egypt:[4] capitation taxes; taxes on land (the huge quantities of grain required for the dole in Rome were extracted from Egypt as a land tax); taxes on produce and animals; taxes on professions and occupations; sales taxes; taxes pertaining to priests and temples; custom taxes and transit taxes. Roman tax collectors specifically collected taxes to cover deficits that occurred when taxpayers fled from their home districts. They mandated taxes to provide for the local prisons and the public baths and to maintain the system of dikes. The Romans also levied taxes for the salaries of the district guards and to underwrite offerings to a new emperor at the beginning of his reign or on occasions such as triumphs and anniversaries. Other taxes of various kinds were also exacted.

As the types of taxes on the preceding list are reflected upon, it becomes evident that at least a portion of these tax revenues benefited the local and regional infrastructure. The collectors did not immediately transport all revenues to Rome. In addition to the system of dikes and the public baths just mentioned, other public works such as amphitheaters benefited the local population. Provincial tax revenues also supported the system of roads for which the Roman empire was famous. Roman achievements with respect to harbors and water supply through aqueducts and other means must also be mentioned in any discussion of infrastructure.

Such forms of public works certainly provided tangible benefits to the peoples of the subjugated territories, even if a concern for the subjugated populace was scarcely a decisive consideration for those who ruled the empire. In effect, these construction projects constituted one of four key elements employed by the Roman authorities in their effort to make Roman rule palatable to those who were the subjects under this rule.

The achievement of relative peace and order, *pax atque quieta,* within the conquered territories was a second key element. The nature of Augustus' peace was that of an imposed peace. It was achieved by military campaigns or the threat of such campaigns, and it was dependent on the continuing deployment of hundreds of thousands of Roman troops. Nevertheless, this form of peace successfully prohibited and quelled regional conflicts, civil strife, and attacks by bandits and pirates. For these reasons many within the province, especially the provincial elites, readily welcomed Augustus' peace.

The effective utilization of these regional and municipal elites was the third key component in Augustus' strategy for achieving an effective administration of Rome's provinces. Apart from special arrangements involving client kings, the authority of the Roman governor now became supreme within a given province. Nevertheless, local authorities, particularly those whose positions were firmly established prior to Augustus, could be authorized to oversee many aspects of daily life, including public order and the collection of taxes. Local magnates who cooperated in fulfilling Roman objectives might well retain and enhance their property holdings, their positions of influence, and their titles of honor. With respect to the Roman province of Judea, various members of the Herodian dynasty and various members of the priestly families who dominated the Jerusalem Sanhedrin are examples of local rulers who functioned effectively within the Roman system and profited thereby.

The coveted grant of Roman citizenship was also made to local authorities who worked cooperatively and enthusiastically to further imperial aims. In effect, these citizenship grants brought those who received them into the realm of privilege customarily enjoyed only by the free inhabitants of Rome and Italy. Members of local elites might also find paths of advancement open to them through the ceremonial priesthoods connected with various regional temples that became centers for the developing cults of Rome and its emperors—particularly Augustus. These forms of imperial advancement were distinct from the "course of honors" (*cursus honorum*) that, in Rome, was open to the members of the senatorial and equestrian orders. Nevertheless, the members of provincial groups who chose to identify themselves with Rome's cause found ample opportunity for establishing their own progress in civic honor.

The fourth key element in Augustus' program was the dissemination of convincing propaganda on behalf of imperial rule. The famous "Altar of Peace" in Rome and other edifices at the provincial level were constructed from a desire to advance public gratitude for the benefits of Roman peace. Similarly, inscriptions on public buildings and the figures and inscriptions engraved on coins stressed that Augustus was a "Benefactor" and "Savior" for those whom he ruled. Further, Roman poets and writers proclaimed the "eternity" (*aeternitas*) of Roman rule. For example, in commenting on Augustus' adoption of Tiberius as his successor, one Roman author announced that this step heralded "the perpetual security and eternity of the Roman empire."

For all of these reasons, the responsible course for all subjugated peoples was to live peacefully and cooperatively under Roman rule. If attempted, uprisings and insurrections were bound to be futile. Attempted alliances with Rome's external enemies (the Parthians to the East, for example) would be doomed to failure. The inevitability of Rome's rule was such that those who were truly wise could only accede to it and respect it. To have each of the preceding statements widely accepted was the goal of Augustus' explicit and implicit propaganda.

THE SITUATION OF AUGUSTUS' SUCCESSORS, ESPECIALLY NERO

Augustus reigned as emperor for an astonishing length of forty-five years. His initiatives during this extended period laid the foundation for Roman domination for centuries to come. In effect, he succeeded in creating a new model for political rule over the empire, an arrangement that provided the reigning emperor with enormous power while respecting, to a degree, the historical prerogatives of the Roman senate.

The model Augustus developed possessed one extremely crucial weakness: its inability to provide for a problem-free succession to the office of emperor. Was there even to be a succession of emperors? Senators who desired a return to the consular patterns of the Republic were not lacking. If rule by a princeps was not rule by a king or dictator, how could the male heirs of a princeps succeed him in office? As noted in the preceding section, Augustus solved the vexing problem of his own immediate successor by adopting Tiberius as his heir and conferring upon him the right of succession. Nevertheless, the problem of succession arose again and again during the remainder of the first century and beyond. In some cases the praetorian guard intervened in the selection proceedings. In some cases Roman generals used the support of their legions to seize the office. Maneuverings by members of the senate were also a factor to be reckoned with in the various struggles over succession.

At this juncture, it is useful to list Augustus' successors during the first Christian century:

> Augustus (31 B.C.–A.D. 14)
> Tiberius (14–37)
> Gaius (37–41)
> Claudius (41–54)
> Nero (54–68)
> Galba/Otho/Vitellius (68–69)
> Vespasian (69–79)
> Titus (79–81)
> Domitian (81–96)
> Nerva (96–98)
> Trajan (98–118)

Two observations can be made concerning the positions achieved by these emperors: (1) they wielded vast power; and (2) they were extremely vulnerable once they reached the imperial throne. As described in the preceding section, Augustus consolidated extensive territories that were rich in both human and natural resources. As a consequence of Augustus' administrative genius, his successors inherited the mechanisms and the structures for controlling and exploiting these resources. An extensive imperial staff consisting principally of members of the equestrian class and emancipated slaves ("freedmen") was now in existence. Even more significantly, an army of legionaries and auxiliaries that numbered approximately three hundred thousand stood ready to implement the emperor's policies and directives.

But those who secured the imperial office in the decades Augustus were not able to wield power and enjoy the benefits power without agitation and turmoil. Consider the experience of these first-century emperors: Tiberius was conspired against by the prefect of the praetorian guard; Gaius was assassinated; Claudius died under circumstances that suggested poisoning; Nero was pressured to suicide by the revolt of key legion commanders and members of the praetorian guard; Galba, Otho, and Vitellius each survived only a few months. Vespasian restored a degree of stability to the imperial office and the transition to the rule of Titus, Vespasian's elder son was smooth. This relative peacefulness was of short duration. Continuous intrigues and frequent conflicts attended the rule of Domitian, Vespasian's second son. Domitian was eventually assassinated in A.D. 96 and the Roman senate promptly damned his memory.

Given these circumstances, it is not surprising that, once they had secured the imperial office, individual emperors utilized various strategies in order to protect themselves and promote the acceptance of their rule. The steps taken by these emperors, aggressively or tacitly, to promote their own "ruler cult" are particularly of interest in the present study. To have temples, sanctuaries, priesthoods, and ceremonies dedicated to extolling the "genius" of the ruling emperor and to have other forms of provincial acclaim for the emperor as quasi divine was useful to virtually every emperor. These practices were especially attractive to emperors such as Gaius, Nero, and Domitian. The degree to which those just named became convinced that they possessed a suprahuman identity is an intriguing issue that cannot be conclusively decided given the existing data. Still, it is significant for the New Testament writings that each of these three rulers accepted deifying accolades and referred to himself in terms bespeaking a quasi-divine status.

If Augustus' successors (Tiberius was possibly an exception) welcomed this developing imperial ruler cult as a means for increasing their popular support, these same emperors utilized new applications of the traditional laws regarding *maiestas* ("treason") as a means of protecting themselves from specific real (or perceived) threats. Originally designed to protect the Roman people from treasonous conduct, laws pertaining to *maiestas* were reinterpreted and reformulated to safeguard the person of the emperor and his immediate family.

Some prosecutions for maiestas accurately targeted potential assassins. Nevertheless, with emperors such as Nero and Domitian, prosecution for maiestas could easily be initiated as a means for dealing with any imagined rival and for stifling any type of criticism. Domitian claimed that an emperor's allegations of maiestas frequently fell upon deaf ears until after the conspiracy had successfully achieved the emperor's demise. Nevertheless, Domitian, along with Nero, was perhaps the most egregious abuser of the maiestas procedures.

Nero's own manipulation of the maiestas laws was reflective of his apparently insatiable desire to be recognized as supreme.[5] This desire led him to seek virtually every title, every honor, every form of acclaim. His callous murder of his mother Agrippina in A.D. 59 was probably a manifestation of this desire for unfettered supremacy. Nero owed his throne to his mother's efforts, machinations that reportedly included the poisoning of her husband, Claudius. Nevertheless, as long as Agrippina remained a force upon the Roman scene, Nero felt that his own power was constrained and diminished.

From a Christian perspective, Nero's barbarity in martyring various Christians in Rome in A.D. 64 represented another low point of his regime. When popular suspicion fell upon him as the arsonist responsible for the fire that devastated a significant part of Rome, Nero sought to divert attention from himself by blaming the Christians of the city. Having selected them as his scapegoats, Nero then proceeded against these Christians in a brutal and savage fashion.

The following narrative is quoted at length because Nero's maleficence may have decisively influenced various New Testament authors. As noted in chapter 1, there is a considerable degree of uncertainty regarding the dates of many of the texts that now comprise the canon. It is thus possible that a significant number of the writers of the New Testament may have been aware of this emperor's cruel and barbarous conduct. Circa A.D. 115, Tacitus, a

Roman senator with noteworthy interests in imperial history,[6] wrote the following account of this earlier heinous event:

> Nero substituted as culprits, and punished with the utmost refinements of cruelty, a class of men, loathed for their vices, whom the crowd styled Christians. Christus, the founder of the name, had undergone the death penalty in the reign of Tiberius, by sentence of the procurator Pontius Pilatus, and the pernicious superstition was checked for a moment, only to break out once more, not merely in Judaea, the home of the disease, but in the capital itself, where all things horrible or shameful in the world collect and find a vogue. First, then, the confessed members of the sect were arrested; next, on their disclosures, vast numbers were convicted, not so much on the count of arson as for hatred of the human race. And derision accompanied their end: they were covered with wild beasts' skins and torn to death by dogs; or they were fastened on crosses, and, when daylight failed were burned to serve as lamps by night. Nero had offered his Gardens for the spectacle, and gave an exhibition in his Circus, mixing with the crowd in the habit of a charioteer, or mounted on his car. Hence, in spite of a guilt which had earned the most exemplary punishment, there arose a sentiment of pity, due to the impression that they were being sacrificed not for the welfare of the state but to the ferocity of a single man. (*Annals* 15.44)

ROMAN RULE NEGATIVELY PORTRAYED

The preceding sections have described the imperial system of Augustus and his successors from the standpoint of its organization and administration. It is now appropriate to consider Roman rule from the perspective of those in the provinces who bitterly resented the imposition of this system upon them.

Because conquered peoples have historically rarely had the possibility for publishing their resentment and resistance toward the powers subjugating them, it is not surprising that the two following references are both the work of writers who had established positions in the upper echelons of the Roman system. The first passage to be considered is another selection from Tacitus. While repulsed by the aberrations of such emperors as Nero and

Domitian, Tacitus was himself sympathetic to Roman imperial objectives. His work *Agricola,* published in A.D. 98, describes the military campaign of the Roman general charged with completing the subjugation of Britain that had originally been begun by Julius Caesar. Despite his own obvious sympathies toward Agricola (Agricola was in fact Tacitus' father-in-law), Tacitus portrays the British chieftain Calgacus, making the following denunciation of the Romans:

> But today the uttermost parts of Britain are laid bare; there are no other tribes to come; nothing but sea and cliffs and these more deadly Romans, whose arrogance you shun in vain by obedience and self-restraint. Harriers of the world, now that earth fails their all-devastating hands, they probe even the sea: if their enemy have wealth, they have greed; if he be poor, they are ambitious; East nor West has glutted them; alone of humankind they behold with the same passion of concupiscence waste alike and want. To plunder, butcher, steal, these things they misname empire: they make a desolation and they call it peace. Children and kin are by the law of nature each man's dearest possessions; they are swept away from us by conscription to be slaves in other lands: our wives and sisters, even when they escape a soldier's lust, are debauched by self-styled friends and guests: our goods and chattels go for tribute; our land and harvests in requisitions of grain; life and limb themselves are used up in levelling marsh and forest to the accompaniment of gibes and blows. (*Agricola* 30–31)

The second set of references also delineates a call to arms for the purpose of opposing Roman rule. The writer in this instance is Josephus, a Jewish general in the revolt of A.D. 66–69 who became a historian sympathetic to the Romans after being captured by them. In presenting accounts of the revolt that generally stress the foolhardiness of challenging Roman power, Josephus still took pains to explain the premises and the motivations of the Zealot leader who initiated violent resistance sixty years earlier. According to Josephus' works *The Jewish War* and *Jewish Antiquities,* Judas the Gaulanite urged resistance to the Roman census (and the taxation associated with it) in the following terms:

> Under his [Coponius'] administration, a Galilean, named Judas, incited his countrymen to revolt, upbraiding them as cowards for

consenting to pay tribute to the Romans and tolerating mortal masters, after having God for their lord. (*Jewish War* 2.8.1)

But a certain Judas, a Gaulanite from a city named Gamala, who had enlisted the aid of Saddok, a Pharisee, threw himself into the cause of rebellion. They said that the assessment carried with it a status amounting to downright slavery, no less, and appealed to the nation to make a bid for independence. They urged that in case of success the Jews would have laid the foundation for prosperity, while if they failed to obtain any such boon, they would win honor and renown for their lofty aim; and that Heaven would be their zealous helper to no lesser end than the furthering of their enterprise until it succeeded—all the more if with high devotion in their hearts they stood firm and did not shrink from the bloodshed that might be necessary. (*Jewish Antiquities* 18.1.1)

Given that the territories of the Roman province of Judea were the site of Jesus' ministry, the violent protest referenced in the immediately preceding paragraph is highly significant. This uprising took place in A.D. 6, and there are grounds for holding that the revolutionary movement of the Zealots continued, at least intermittently, during the lifetime of Jesus. In A.D. 66, the resistance initiated by Judas came to full expression when Jewish partisans under the leadership of one of Judas' sons defeated the Roman legion assigned to the province. This initial military success resulted in a brief period of autonomy, which included the restoration of a high priest of the Zadokite lineage.[7]

Bearing in mind considerations about the various aspects of Roman rule described in the preceding sections, it is now appropriate to move to a systematic analysis of Luke's presentation of Jesus' ministry within Roman-dominated Judea, supplemented by references from Mark and Matthew. Chapter 4 will then analyze the perspective of the Gospel of John.

NOTES

1. See R. Cassidy, *Jesus, Politics, and Society: A Study of Luke's Gospel* (Maryknoll, N.Y.: Orbis Books, 1978); *Society and Politics in the Acts of the Apostles* (Maryknoll, N.Y.: Orbis Books, 1983); *John's Gospel*

in New Perspective: Christology and the Realities of Roman Power (Maryknoll, N.Y.: Orbis Books, 1992). See also my forthcoming study, *Paul in Chains: The Impact of Roman Imprisonment in the Letters of Paul* (New York: Crossroad, 2001).

2. The absence of slavery, in the normal meaning of that term, from the Jewish territories of Palestine is significant as an explanation for the lack of any explicit critique of slavery within the Gospel accounts of Jesus' teachings. See Cassidy, *Jesus, Politics, and Society*, 34–39, 111–13.

3. The status of Philippi as one such Roman colony is significant for the interpretation of Paul's letter to the Philippians as well as for the interpretation of Acts 16.

4. See the valuable study by S. Wallace, *Taxation in Egypt from Augustus to Diocletian* (Princeton: Princeton University Press, 1938).

5. Chapter 5 of my *Paul in Chains* contains a section on *maiestas* under Nero. That Paul would have been ultimately condemned by Nero on this charge is suggested in chapter 10 of the same study.

6. As the phrase "the pernicious superstition" in the second sentence of this excerpt indicates, Tacitus himself was no friend of the Christian movement.

7. The significance of this step is explicated in my *Jesus, Politics, and Society*, 116. In effect, then, Annas, Caiphas, and the others who reacted so violently to Jesus' temple protest did not have a legitimate succession to the office of high priest. See pp. 20–25 below for additional ramifications.

3

Jesus and Roman Rule
in the Synoptic Gospels

HIS CHAPTER WILL INTRODUCE comparisons between Jesus'
approach to social relations (the "humility-service model")
and the approach of the Roman authorities (the "domination model"). Luke, more than Mark or Matthew, provides an
extensive range of reports situating Jesus' ministry with reference
to Roman rule.[1] After Luke's reports have been assimilated, significant reports from Mark and Matthew that are not contained in
Luke will be considered. Finally, a brief section will characterize
Luke's own personal outlook regarding Roman rule.

SITUATING LUKE'S JESUS
IN ROMAN JUDEA

Luke considers it important to inform his readers regarding the
political arrangements that were in effect at the birth of Jesus
(2:1–7) and those that were in effect when Jesus began his public
ministry (3:1–2). Significantly, this latter passage identifies all of
the following: the reigning Roman emperor, Tiberius, the current
Roman governor of Judea, Pontius Pilate, and the members of the
local elites who operated under the Roman umbrella, namely,
Herod Antipas, Herod Philip, Lysanias, Annas, and Caiaphas.

Further, as the Gospel narrative unfolds, Luke portrays Jesus as knowledgeable about the key components of Roman rule in Judea and its surrounding territories. Jesus' social conduct within the setting of this imperial rule will be considered below. The emphasis here is on the fact that Luke's Jesus is familiar with the violent practices of Pontius Pilate (13:1–3), the treachery of Herod Antipas (13:31–33), and the effrontery and exploitation of the chief priests of the Jerusalem temple (19:45–46; 20:9–18). Further, Luke's Jesus recognizes the characteristic dominating practices of the Roman rulers and their fascination with "benefactor" as a title of honor (22:24–25).

There are also several Lukan attestations of Jesus' familiarity with Roman taxation. Jesus initially made one tax collector a key disciple (5:27–32), later commended the conversion of a chief tax collector (19:1–10), and was himself criticized for associating with tax collectors (7:34; 15:1–2). Jesus' response in the famous tribute passage (20:20–26) also testifies to his awareness of the emperor's powers to mint coins and to require taxes.

Significantly Luke also portrays Jesus in close association with at least one member of the Zealot movement, the apostle Simon (6:15; also Acts 1:13). This indicates Jesus' familiarity with the approach of those utilizing revolutionary violence against Roman rule. Indeed in 23:2, the chief priests allege that Jesus himself is within the Zealot camp.

THE HUMILITY-SERVICE APPROACH OF LUKE'S JESUS

Since leading characteristics of the Roman system have been described in chapter 2, it is now appropriate to consider the leading characteristics of the humility-service model that Luke's Jesus espouses. It is remarkable (and the rationale for the name of this model) that Luke's Jesus repeatedly instructs his disciples on the topics of service and humility. In both the ninth and twenty-second chapters, Luke indicates that disputes arose among the disciples as to which of them was the greatest. In chapter 9 Luke reports that Jesus took a child to his side and stated that the response that any of them gave to such a child was a measure of their greatness. He concluded this intervention with the words, "for he who is least among you all is the one who is great" (9:48b).

Another dispute over greatness took place at the time of Jesus' final supper:

> A dispute also arose among them, which of them was to be regarded as the greatest. And he [Jesus] said to them, "The kings of the Gentiles exercise lordship over them; and those in authority over them are called benefactors. But not so with you; rather let the greatest among you become as the youngest, and the leader as one who serves. For which is the greater, one who sits at table, or one who serves? Is it not the one who sits at table? But I am among you as one who serves." (22:24–27)

In these two instances, Jesus' emphasis on humility and service was in response to a quarrel over rank and position. Luke portrays Jesus upholding humility and service in other contexts as well. Positively, in 17:7–10, Jesus instructs the disciples regarding a dedicated service that does not require thanks. Indeed, those who render such authentic service should consider it no more than their duty.

Negatively, in 11:43, Luke reports Jesus' criticism of the Pharisees for seeking the best seats in the synagogues and salutation in the marketplaces. Jesus makes a similar criticism of the scribes in 20:45–47, citing them for the above practices, for wearing long robes and making long prayers for the sake of pretense, and for seeking the best seats at banquets.

The parable that Luke's Jesus relates in 14:1–7 also criticizes this type of behavior. Luke indicates that Jesus told this parable after he had observed guests choosing the places of honor at a banquet. The closing words of this parable are similar to those expressed by Jesus in one of his earlier admonitions to the disciples (see 9:48b): "For every one who exalts himself will be humbled, and he who humbles himself will be exalted" (14:11). Four chapters later (18:9–14), the parable of the Pharisee and tax collector also concludes with virtually the same admonition. Further, in the parable proper, the Pharisee's self-righteousness is scored and the humility of the tax collector is praised.

These teachings on humility and service can be compared with the *cursus honorum* ("course of honors"), which was designed to prepare members of the Roman elite for their roles in exercising power within the empire, but the contrast could scarcely be more marked. A similar kind of contrast also emerges when Jesus' teaching regarding the importance of care for the poor and the infirm is juxtaposed with the characteristic Roman view regarding the despoiling and enslavement of those conquered. How strange to the ears of those attuned to Roman values, this parable by Luke's Jesus:

> He said also to the man who had invited him, "When you give a dinner or a banquet, do not invite your friends or your brothers or your kinsmen or rich neighbors, lest they also invite you in return, and you be repaid. But when you give a feast, invite the poor, the maimed, the lame, the blind, and you will be blessed, because they cannot repay you. You will be repaid at the resurrection of the just." (14:12–14)

This passage is far from the only instance in which Jesus calls for material resources to be used on behalf of the poor and the lowly. Indeed, as even a casual reading of Luke's Gospel discloses, Jesus repeatedly calls for surplus possessions to be distributed for the benefit of the poor. Significantly, the only case in which a rich person received commendation from Jesus is in the instance of Zacchaeus *after* Zacchaeus announced a startling initiative to right past injustices and to share radically with the poor (19:1–9).

In addition to the concern that Luke portrays Jesus expressing for the poor and the infirm, the evangelist also shows Jesus giving affirmation to several other groups that were less regarded in the prevailing social context. Among the groups that fall into this category are Samaritans, Gentiles, women, tax collectors, and sinners.

With its emphasis on concern for the poor and the lowly and its emphasis on service and humility, Jesus' approach contrasts strikingly with any domination-oriented approach. Nevertheless, according to Luke's Gospel, it was not for any of these convictions that Jesus received the sentence of crucifixion from the Roman governor of Judea. According to Luke's account, Jesus' most basic conflict with the social order maintained by Rome in the province of Judea occurred when Jesus arrived in Jerusalem and made an aggressive attack upon the chief priests, who were accredited by Rome for the administration of the Jewish temple and the control of the Jerusalem Sanhedrin.

In his protest at the temple (19:45–46), Jesus quoted the prophet Isaiah to proclaim that, under the reigning chief priests, the temple had become "a den of robbers." His action complemented and reinforced these words: "he began to drive out those who sold." Jesus' passion and assertiveness are fundamental dimensions of the scene Luke depicts. Nevertheless, this prophetic intervention is made without the use of weapons and is fundamentally non-violent in character. Jesus, in effect, accomplishes a dramatic protest without physically injuring any individual.

The same qualities of assertiveness and nonviolence character-ize Jesus' engagements with the chief priests and their allies in the scenes that follow next. After effectively countering the chief priests' challenge regarding his own credentials (20:1–8), Jesus resumed his attack on them with a forceful parable identifying them as "wicked tenants" who would be vanquished as the vine-yard was taken from them (20:9–18). When it is recognized that the four priestly families then controlling the temple and the San-hedrin were not authentic priests in terms of Zadokite lineage, this parable can be regarded as constituting a profound threat to them.[2]

Luke's next report emphasizes that the parable had the effect of galvanizing this group into action against Jesus (20:19): "The scribes and chief priests tried to lay hands on him at that very hour, but they feared the people; for they perceived that he had told this parable against them." Luke then describes the strategy that the chief priests evolved for eradicating Jesus: "So they watched him, and sent spies, who pretended to be sincere, that they might take hold of what he said, so as to deliver him up to the authority and jurisdiction of the governor" (20:20).

A little more than a day later, with Judas' assistance, the chief priests and their guards apprehended Jesus, brought him before Pilate, and denounced him on the grounds that he was challenging Roman rule as a Zealot: "And they began to accuse him saying, 'we found this man perverting our nation, and forbidding us to give

tribute to Caesar, and saying that he himself is Christ a king'"
(23:2). These were fundamentally false charges. For according to
Luke's Gospel, Jesus was far from being a Zealot. Indeed, arguing
from Luke's account, a strong case can be made that Jesus consciously and decisively rejected the decision of the Zealots to take
up arms against their Roman enemies.

It is important to recognize that Jesus' teachings regarding love
and forgiveness were not restricted to the Zealots in their applica-
tion. In fact, these teachings pertain to Jesus' social context in
three principal ways. Positively, these teachings serve to delineate
the character of the relations Jesus strove to bring about among his
disciples. Negatively, these teachings represent a criticism of *both*
the Roman approach and the Zealot approach. When Jesus teaches
in Luke 6:27–28, "But I say to you that hear, love your enemies, do
good to those who hate you, pray for those who abuse you," these
words challenge the Romans in their penchant for conquering and
often annihilating those who oppose their designs. At the same
time, they confront the program of the Zealots for repulsing and
destroying the Roman forces. In similar fashion, Jesus' teaching on
forgiveness in Luke 17:3–4 has applications on both the Roman
and Zealot fronts.

It has sometimes been suggested that Luke portrays Jesus relax-
ing his teachings against the use of the sword in his penultimate
instructions to his disciples. Without close analysis, Jesus' words
and his disciples' response in 22:35–38 can suggest such a conclusion. Yet, when this passage is carefully considered, Luke is actually portraying the disciples' obtuse failure to understand Jesus'
metaphorical meaning in speaking about the need for a sword.

Luke initially relates that Jesus responded with marked exas-
peration over the disciples' failure to apprehend his meaning. The
next sequence of events and words in Luke's narrative is of decisive significance for a correct appreciation of Jesus' stance in
adamantly rejecting the means of violence:

> While he was still speaking, there came a crowd, and the man called
> Judas, one of the twelve, was leading them. He drew near to Jesus to
> kiss him; but Jesus said to him, "Judas, would you betray the Son of
> man with a kiss?" And when those who were about him saw what
> would follow, they said, "Lord, shall we strike with the sword? And

one of them struck the slave of the high priest and cut off his right ear. But Jesus said, "No more of this!" And he touched his ear and healed him. (22:47–51)

Before treating the issue of Jesus' stance on the volatile issue of Roman taxation, attention must be given to Luke's characterization of Jesus as frequently in prayerful communication with God. Luke depicts Jesus as deeply engaged in personal prayer on the occasion of his baptism, many times during his public ministry, and at the time of his death on the cross. Luke also indicates that Jesus encouraged his disciples to pray and gave them the "Lord's Prayer" as a model when they asked him for guidance in how to pray. In summary, it is through prayer that Luke's Jesus seeks to stand in faithful communication with the Father regarding the Father's purposes.

The numerous instances in which "the kingdom of God" is a reference point within the Gospel strengthen the impression that Luke's Jesus adopts God's concerns as his paramount priority. Luke often portrays Jesus describing what the kingdom of God is like and how it arrives. It is, in effect, the central concept that he uses in describing the thrust of his ministry (4:43; 9:60; 16:16; 22:16, 18). These references to God's kingdom are buttressed and enhanced by Jesus' words explicating that God's indisputable sovereignty and power provide the foundation for the radical teaching regarding love of enemies (6:35–36). Similarly, God's sovereign power and benevolence provide the warrant for Jesus' teachings about possessions and a person's security (12:22–31).

JESUS VIS-À-VIS ROMAN TAXATION AND THE ROMAN ORDER

The foregoing considerations relative to God's sovereignty are essential to the correct interpretation of Jesus' stance toward the Roman authorities in Luke and to the correct interpretation of Jesus' nuanced position regarding Roman taxes. For purposes of exposition, it is useful to treat Jesus' reply to the tribute question within the context of his other words concerning the Roman authorities and their allies. Jesus' appreciation for God's sovereignty and his allegiance to God's concerns constitute the background for all of these responses.

In 13:31 Jesus accepts a report that Herod Antipas, the Roman-appointed ruler of Galilee, intends to kill him. His reply in 13:32–33 is as follows: "Go and tell that fox, 'Behold, I cast out demons and perform cures today and tomorrow, and the third day I finish my course. Nevertheless, I must go on my way today and tomorrow and the day following.'" In essence, Jesus' words in this passage indicate his allegiance to the course that has been given to him by God. He will not be intimidated by the murderous threats of a Roman ruler like Herod Antipas if that ruler's objectives are inconsistent with the course that Jesus "must" follow. In this instance, Jesus is far from being subject to Herod Antipas. Nor does he accord him a conventional honorific. Instead he disparagingly refers to him as "that fox."[3]

The concept of maintaining allegiance to one's course despite persecution by the political authorities is present also in Jesus' words to the disciples in chapter 21. Jesus is addressing them concerning a time of great upheavals (21:12–15), and he indicates that they can expect to be handed over to "synagogues and prisons" and brought before "kings and governors." When this happens they are not to waver or become fearful about their witness to Jesus' name. Rather they are to stand firm in their testimony, and Jesus himself will give them a wisdom that none of their adversaries will be able to withstand.

A passage that has already been referred to in a previous section also has relevance in this context. In Luke 22:24–27, Jesus indicates to the disciples that they must not be influenced by the domination-oriented practices of the political authorities around them. In showing him trying to keep the disciples from being seduced by this "domination model," Luke once again portrays a Jesus whose own approach is not influenced by the behavioral patterns of the surrounding political authorities.

The series of responses that Luke depicts Jesus making at the time of his trials also serves to indicate that Jesus does not automatically defer to the political rulers appointed by the emperor or to the procedures these authorities were accustomed to following.

Luke portrays Jesus on trial before the Jerusalem Sanhedrin, before the Roman prefect, Pilate, and before Herod Antipas. He shows Jesus making slightly different responses in each of these venues, but at no time does he portray Jesus taking particular account of the high political offices held by those who interrogated and judged him.

In the first part of the trial before Pilate, Luke reports that, after Pilate heard the three charges brought by the members of the Sanhedrin, he asked Jesus a single question: "Are you the King of the Jews?" (23:3). Though Pilate held worldly power of life and death, Jesus' reply was terse and nondeferential: "You have said so" (23:3). As Luke describes the scene before Herod Antipas, Jesus was even less cooperative: "So he questioned him at some length; but he made no answer" (23:9).

In the remainder of the trial before Pilate, Luke does not report that Pilate asked Jesus any further questions, nor that Jesus volunteered any comments to Pilate or any of the others who were present. Jesus' participation in the trials before Pilate and Herod Antipas was thus minimal. He answered tersely and noncommittally to Pilate's single question, and to Herod's questions he answered not at all.

Jesus' teaching on the subject of Roman taxation is cut from the same cloth as his prediction of persecution by kings and governors and his refusal to be swayed from his own course by Herod's threats. It is cut from the same cloth as his conduct at his political trials and his admonition that his disciples reject the patterns of those authorities who dominate over their subjects. As Luke presents them, each of these responses involves, to some degree, the elements of sovereignty and allegiance. The same two elements are centrally present in Jesus' response to the question put to him by the chief priests' spies regarding the payment of Roman taxes.

Did Jesus himself pay Roman tribute? It should be cautioned at the outset that Luke 20:20-26 will not provide a yes or no answer to this question—which is not to imply that this passage is silent regarding Jesus' perspective regarding the Roman order and the claims of Caesar. For, in effect, Jesus gives a substantive pronouncement on the subject of Roman taxation even though he does not disclose his own practice.

An initial point to emphasize is that no passage in the Gospel of Luke portrays Jesus teaching or operating "dualistically," that is, as though there were *two* realms to be respected, God's and Caesar's. The passages pertaining to God's sovereignty and the kingdom of God that were cited in the preceding section establish that Luke's Jesus envisions and acts in terms of only one realm, a realm created by God and a realm in which God is ultimately sovereign. For Luke's Jesus there is no other realm that is independent of God's realm. Only one creation exists, and God alone is sovereign over all creation. Given these considerations, it is thus a serious mistake to set forth a dualistic interpretation of the present passage. Unfortunately, such a line of interpretation has been followed all too frequently.

A second interpretative approach also frequently functions to keep the powerful meaning of Jesus' reply from being correctly apprehended. In this second approach, attention is concentrated on Jesus' strategy in requesting a denarius and eliciting from his questioners that Caesar's likeness and Caesar's inscription were imprinted upon it. Jesus' request may indeed have functioned to expose the bad faith of the spies in posing their question. Nevertheless, to concentrate only on this aspect is to fail to uncover the full meaning of Jesus' reply. After the spies had disclosed that a denarius was in their possession, Jesus pronounced the following memorable words: "Then render to Caesar, the things that are Caesar's and to God the things that are God's" (20:25).

The interpretation of this pronouncement that will now be presented can be characterized as "the evaluation interpretation." It is an interpretation that is closely tied to what has been explicated above regarding Jesus' espousal of a service-humility approach to social relationships. In effect, the careful wording of Jesus' reply to the spies' question calls for reflection and dialogue regarding "Caesar's things" and regarding "God's things." The outcome of this reflection and dialogue will be an "evaluation" of the things of Caesar in light of the things of God. This evaluation must precede any decision on the specific question of paying or refusing the imperial taxes.

What "things" truly belong to Caesar? That is the first question to be addressed in the process of reaching a final judgment about the payment of the imperial tax. Harbors, roads, aqueducts, gymnasiums, treasuries, soldiers, territory: do any of these things ultimately belong to Caesar? No, in the perspective of Jesus all such items and all other *realia* ultimately belong to God as sovereign creator. Caesar, for all of his accrued power and honor, does not hold autonomous title to any of these "things." Caesar is rather called to be the steward of God regarding those things that he temporarily and contingently administers.

The second clause of Jesus' pronouncement essentially functions to repeat and reinforce the meaning that is already contained in the first clause. In effect, Jesus directs attention to those things that are "God's things." But what does not belong to God? All gifts of nature and all of the artifices of human construction ultimately belong to God. Further, God's "things" also encompass such attributes as humility, service, sharing with the poor, nonviolence—in short, everything that pertains to the service-humility model that Jesus has been espousing. God's "things" also include prayer, worship, and spiritual practices such as fasting. Nevertheless, it would be a grave mistake (yet one frequently made) to restrict "the things of God" only to the latter items.

Once it is recognized that Caesar holds nothing autonomously and that God holds all things with full sovereignty, the way is open for responding properly to Caesar's demand for taxes. Since Caesar is, in effect, temporarily the steward of God, his stewardship must be evaluated in terms of God's concerns and purposes for humanity and for all of creation. If Caesar is proving to be a reliable steward in terms of those things that God would have accomplished, then taxes may appropriately be given in support of Caesar's stewardship. However, if Caesar's policies and practices are antithetical to the things that God desires, then no obligation exists to pay the demanded taxes.

In effect, then, all who are faced with Caesar's demand for taxes must first evaluate Caesar's rule against the standards of God's concerns before deciding to pay or refuse the imperial taxes. Are God's concerns and God's priorities being advanced by Caesar's policies and practices? If the answer to this question is yes, then the way is open for compliance with the demanded taxes. And conversely.

At this juncture it is important to explicate precisely the relationship between two of the terms that have been used in the preceding paragraphs. The "humility-service model" designates Jesus' fundamental approach to social and political relationships. The "evaluation approach" distinctly designates Jesus' way of responding to the social and political order of imperial Rome.

Throughout his public ministry Jesus, according to Luke, taught and lived according to the humility-service model, a social model that contrasted fundamentally with the domination model of imperial Rome. When asked to respond to the Roman model (specifically to the taxes that the Roman leaders demanded), Jesus' approach was to insist that it be evaluated in terms of "the things of God." In giving this response, Jesus was not thereby proposing any specific alternative form of government. (In terms of the existing realities of Palestine, Jesus' call for evaluation did not imply endorsement for the model of political rule proposed by the Zealots.) In principle, any form of government was to be subject to evaluation with reference to God's purposes. In this specific situation, the questioners sought to elicit his response to *Roman* rule. His reply was of such a character that it might potentially be applied to any other form of political rule.[4]

One additional clarification regarding Jesus' approach to Roman rule can be achieved by posing the question of whether Luke's Jesus could be considered dangerous, in some sense, to Roman provincial rule. The answer to this question involves a judgment about the potential for the humility-service model to undermine the social premises of the domination model. Further it involves a judgment about the potential of a social movement that rejects the use of violence to overcome a power for whom violent measures and the threat of violent measures are watchwords. In his trial narrative Luke makes it clear that Pilate did not actually consider Jesus a threat to the Roman order (Pilate was, however, prepared to execute Jesus out of expedience). Nevertheless, presuming numerous converts to Jesus' "way," there are substantive grounds for concluding that Pilate misapprehended the power of Jesus' approach in considering that Jesus posed no threat to Roman rule.[5]

HUMILITY, SERVICE, AND TAXATION
IN MARK AND MATTHEW

Because Luke's Gospel shows manifold signs of its author's desire to portray the Roman context in which Jesus exercised his ministry, it has been the focus of attention up until this point. In the section that now follows, abbreviated attention will be given to the portraits of Jesus that are presented by Mark and by Matthew. In this discussion, attention will be given to three passages in Mark and Matthew that either do not occur in Luke or are not in central focus there.

Can it be asserted with justification that, in its essential portrayal of Jesus, Mark's Gospel depicts him espousing a humility-service model of social conduct? Space limitations militate against a sustained textual analysis of Mark's account, yet it can be answered succinctly that the leading elements of the humility-service model are present in Mark.

Mark emphasizes other dimensions of Jesus' ministry and presents various elements that he has in common with Luke in his own distinctive fashion.[6] Nevertheless, Mark's Jesus teaches humility, expresses compassion for the poor and the sick, affirms other less-regarded groups, counsels the sharing of possessions, and vigorously attacks the chief priests for corruption and exploitation. Mark's Jesus also instructs his disciples regarding the benchmark of service and counsels them to reject the patterns of the Gentile rulers who dominate over their subjects (10:41–45). In Mark, Jesus' response to the treacherous question regarding Roman tribute is essentially the same as that indicated by Luke. Mark also portrays Jesus warning his disciples that they will be arraigned before "governors and kings" for the sake of his name.

Mark's extended account of the beheading of John the Baptist in 6:14–29 is an important passage. Far more than Luke (3:20; 9:7–9) and in greater detail than Matthew (14:1–12), Mark portrays the prophetic baptizer of Jesus undergoing a brutal, capricious death at the hand of the Roman ruler of Galilee. According to Mark, John the Baptist criticized Herod Antipas' marital improprieties and suffered imprisonment and then death for this prophetic denunciation. In the end, John's testimony regarding "the things of God" caused this political ruler to treat John's life as though it was a trifle or a bauble. Jesus' disciples in the imperial capital were treated just as brutally and cavalierly by Nero when he used them as human torches to light the roadside.[7]

The leading elements of the Lukan Jesus' humility-service model are also present in Matthew. As in Mark, Matthew's portrayal of Jesus has its own proper elements and emphases and is distinct from Luke's portrayal. Nevertheless, the various forms of social concern that are predicated of Jesus in Luke and in Mark are predicated of him in Matthew. There are two passages from Matthew that particularly merit discussion here.

The contrast between the humility-service approach of the Synoptic Jesus and the approach represented by the Roman *cursus honorum* is perhaps nowhere better dramatized that in the proclamation of final judgment by Matthew's Jesus. Here it is said that the type of compassionate service that is central to Jesus' approach (and antithetical to the Roman approach) will be decisively upheld when all human conduct is assessed. With reference to Paul's imprisonment, discussed in chapter 7 below, it should be noted that Jesus identifies himself personally with prisoners (as well as with those in other circumstances of deprivation). The salient part of Matthew's extended passage is as follows:

> "For I was hungry and you gave me food, I was thirsty and you gave me drink, I was a stranger and you welcomed me, I was naked and you clothed me, I was sick and you visited me, I was in prison and you came to me." Then the righteous will answer him, "Lord, when did we see thee hungry and feed thee, or thirsty and give thee drink? And when did we see thee a stranger and welcome thee, or naked and clothe thee? And when did we see thee sick or in prison and visit thee?" And the King will answer them, "Truly, I say to you, as you did it to one of the least of these my brethren, you did it to me." (Matt. 25:35–40)

The second passage from Matthew is less well known, and less well interpreted, than the final-judgment passage just considered. Traditionally, Matthew 17:24–27 has been viewed as a pericope pertaining to the issue of taxation for the temple in Jerusalem. Yet once it is recognized that the Romans levied a variety of taxes at the *didrachma* level and that observant Jews were expected to make a yearly *contribution* to the temple (this expected contribution was not a tax), one can view Jesus' reply as another instance of his teaching concerning Roman taxation.[8]

In Matthew 22:21–22, Jesus' teaching after his opponents had produced a Roman denarius was: "Render therefore to Caesar the things that are Caesar's and to God the things that are God's." The dialogue and reflection that such a response required have been emphasized above. Here *Roman* taxes are again at issue, and Jesus' response is cut from the same cloth. After distancing himself from Peter's affirmative reply, he makes the following pronouncement:

> And when he came home, Jesus spoke to him first, saying, "What do you think, Simon? From whom do kings of the earth take toll or tribute? From their sons or from others?" And when he said, "From others," Jesus said to him, "Then the sons are free." (Matt. 17:25b–26)

Jesus' words here also require reflection and dialogue. For what direct bearing do the elliptical, poetic words "Then the sons are free" have on the issue at hand? It is not possible to deduce from them any unqualified answer regarding compliance with Roman taxation. Nor is it possible to determine from this answer whether Jesus himself is regularly in compliance with Roman tax demands. As this pericope continues in v. 27, Jesus does provide for an ad hoc payment. Nevertheless, the miraculous means by which the payment is made from a coin that neither Jesus nor Peter possesses underscores the unique character of this particular payment and suggests that a precedent is not thereby established.

Matthew 17:24–27 is thus consistent with the portrayal of Jesus' approach to Roman rule that is given elsewhere in the Synoptic accounts. On the topic of Roman taxation, Jesus' answers cannot be reduced to a simple affirmative or negative. Rather his replies implicitly point to the necessity of further dialogue. Jesus is not anti-Roman in the manner of the Zealots, yet his approach is profoundly at variance with the Roman model of domination. In the Synoptic Gospels, on the specific issue of Roman taxation, Jesus never provides the unqualified compliance that Roman policy requires.

A NOTE REGARDING
LUKE'S OWN PERSPECTIVE

Until recently substantive numbers of Lukan scholars have expressed or repeated the view that one of Luke's purposes was to win a favorable response from the Roman authorities relative to the new Christian community. That is, Luke wrote to present a "political apologetic." Other scholars, less numerous, have argued that Luke wrote to encourage his fellow Christians to adopt a favorable view of the imperial authorities and their system. That is, Luke wrote to present an "ecclesial apologetic." The perspective of the present study is that *both* of these views misapprehend Luke's true commitment and his true purposes.[9]

Rather, as discussed above, Luke's Gospel presents Jesus challenging the social and political patterns around him and counseling an evaluation of "the things of Caesar" prior to any payment of Roman taxes. Similarly, it will be indicated below in chapter 5 that Acts portrays the Jerusalem disciples and Paul himself adopting a comparable stance in the social and political contexts in which they found themselves. Luke in fact presents a remarkable "chain of disruption" occurring as Jesus' disciples manifest adherence to Jesus' humility-service model and to Jesus as Lord. Indeed, the book of Acts nearly overflows with controversies involving Paul and the imperial authorities.

Does Luke include a surfeit of reports concerning Paul's testimony before various political officials as a means of providing a resource for any of his readers who might find themselves involved in controversies with the Roman authorities? In movingly describing Paul's great faithfulness as a chained prisoner, does Luke intend to strengthen his readers for their own faithfulness under conditions of adversity? Posing questions such as these helps to focus attention on the fact that Luke *extensively* portrays Paul suffering for political considerations.

How does Luke portray individual Roman officials and the Roman system itself within his two volumes? The Lukan Gospel and Acts essentially presume the operation of the Roman system without expressing any particular enthusiasm for it. The Roman landscape is simply a given. Luke's portrayal of Roman officials is also far from adulatory. Some of these officials are indeed depicted favorably: two centurions and the governor Sergius Paulus respond favorably to the Christian message; the centurion Julius treats prisoner Paul considerately. Other ranking officials, however, are depicted as unprincipled, prejudiced, or corrupt: Pilate himself lacks conviction; the governors Felix and Festus both seek personal advantage in presiding over Paul's case; the proconsul Lucius Gallio operates from an anti-Jewish bias.

Before concluding this section another distinct dimension of Luke's perspective must be considered. This dimension is reflected in the striking claim that Luke attributes to Satan as this tempter strives to divert Jesus from his appointed mission:

> And the devil took him up, and showed him all the kingdoms of the world in a moment of time, and said to him, "To you I will give all this authority and their glory; for it has been delivered to me, and I give it to whom I will" (Luke 4:5–6)

Luke presents the devil's claims and artifices in stronger terms that Matthew does in his comparable passage on Jesus' temptation. In including these words, what did Luke want to communicate to readers who, like himself, resided within the Roman empire? Unmistakably, Satan's boast that he orchestrates the power of *all* kingdoms implies the claim that he directs and manipulates the Roman authorities. Luke's inclusion of this passage must have provided his readers with much to ponder, especially if any of them were familiar with the perspective of the author of the book of Revelation.[10] (See chapter 8 below for Revelation's articulation of Roman rule as satanic.) Along with Luke's two identifications (Luke 6:15; Acts 1:13) of the apostle Simon *as a Zealot,* Luke 4:5–6 decisively confirms the futility of all attempts to attribute "political apologetic" to Luke.

NOTES

1. In its principal lines, the interpretation presented in this chapter reflects the analysis made in R. Cassidy, *Jesus, Politics, and Society: A Study of Luke's Gospel* (Maryknoll, N.Y.: Orbis Books, 1978).

2. In effect, Jesus' protest at the temple represented an attack upon these priests as corrupt. By announcing that "the vineyard" will be taken away from them because they are "wicked tenants," Jesus seemingly attacks them in a second area of vulnerability: their lack of legitimate hereditary credentials for the office of high priest.

3. See B. Green, *Like a Tree Planted: An Exploration of Psalms and Parables Through Metaphors* (Collegeville, Minn.: Liturgical Press, 1997), 12–18, for a particularly insightful discussion of the derogatory meaning encompassed by the metaphor "that fox."

4. The continuing relevance of this reply for Christians of the third millennium will be elaborated in chapter 9 below, pp. 132–35.

5. That Jesus' approach, even though it was nonviolent in character, would have undermined Roman rule if it were widely adopted is argued in my *Jesus, Politics, and Society,* 77–82.

6. The question of how Luke may have used Mark's Gospel as a source is prescinded from here. What is fundamentally asserted is that significant numbers of second-century Christians would have had access to the Gospels of Mark, Matthew, and Luke. In all of these Gospels, these disciples would have encountered a portrayal of Jesus espousing a model based upon service and humility. The principal features of this model are evident in Mark and Matthew even though Luke (whatever his process of composition) has presented this model most comprehensively.

7. See Tacitus' account of this deed above in chapter 2.

8. This analysis follows from R. Cassidy, "Matthew 17:24–27—A Word on Civil Taxes," *Catholic Biblical Quarterly* 41 (1979): 571–80.

9. The grounds for rejecting the "political apologetic" approach and the "ecclesial apologetic" approach are presented more comprehensively in R. Cassidy, *Society and Politics in the Acts of the Apostles* (Maryknoll, N.Y.: Orbis Books, 1983), 145–57.

10. It is intriguing to consider whether the author of Luke 4:5–6 and the author of Revelation 13 were ever in direct personal contact. (As discussed in chapter 9 below, early Christian communities must have possessed both of these *texts,* as well as others, at some point in time.) The lack of any firm basis for establishing such a connection, and many similar connections, is what has prompted the present study's methodological emphasis on finished texts and its relative lack of emphasis on dates of composition.

4

John's Gospel and Roman Power

T HE PRESENT CHAPTER TREATS Jesus' response to Roman power according to the Fourth Gospel and the perspective of the final author of the Fourth Gospel (hereafter referred to as "John") regarding Roman rule.[1] Two of the methodological premises enunciated in chapter 1 bear repeating here. The present study undertakes to analyze the texts of the various New Testament writers in their canonical form. Further, no position is taken on the much-debated questions concerning whether John's Gospel reached its final, circulating form earlier than one or more of the Synoptic Gospels.

THE SOVEREIGNTY OF JESUS IN JOHN'S GOSPEL

From its beginning in 1:1 to its concluding author's note in 21:25, the Gospel of John is permeated with insights and emphases pertaining to the sovereignty of Jesus. John's prologue testifies to the Word's preexistence with God and affirms that the Word was God. From the outset of Jesus' public ministry, John portrays Jesus claiming and evidencing an unsurpassed status in his discourse and in his ability to penetrate the recesses of the human heart. Further, as his ministry unfolds, Jesus performs a series of "signs" that demonstrate his sovereign power over nature and over disease. In a seventh and culminating sign, the raising of Lazarus in chapter eleven, Jesus manifests his power over death itself.

It is difficult to overstate how thoroughly John's Gospel is imbued with the sovereignty of Jesus. With respect to Judaism, for example, Jesus himself supersedes and/or reembodies all of the hallowed figures and institutions of the past. Overall, his status and power are such that no human person or human power is able to compare with him or rival him. His sovereign power may be compared only with the sovereign power of the Father, who has sent Jesus, and the sovereign power of the Holy Spirit, the Paraclete, whom Jesus will send at the time of his own departure.

JESUS' PERSPECTIVE ON ROMAN KINGSHIP AND PILATE'S POWER

The preceding considerations regarding Jesus' sovereignty are critical for a correct interpretation of Jesus' pronouncements regarding Roman rule at the time of his trial before Pontius Pilate. In terms of literary context, the first of Jesus' pronouncements comes after Pilate's initial interrogation. Pilate first asked Jesus: "Are you the king of the Jews?" (18:33b). Jesus' assertive, even abrasive, response to Pilate's query was: "Do you say this of your own accord, or did others say it to you about me?" (18:34). Pilate in turn disdainfully brushed this response aside (18:35) and renewed his interrogation with the question, "What have you done?" At this juncture Jesus declares: "My kingship is not of this world; if my kingship were of this world, my servants would fight that I not be handed over to the Jews; but my kingship is not from the world" (18:36).

In the A-B-A' structure of this pronouncement, the first and third clauses express essentially the same idea: that Jesus' own rule is distinct from the kingship or rule that is "of the world" or "from the world." Jesus does not deny having kingship or rule. (That he does have kingship is indeed part of the theme of his overarching sovereignty in the Gospel of John.) His emphasis is rather that his kingship is distinct from other "worldly" kingships.

The center clause of Jesus' reply supplies the rationale for this distinction: Jesus' kingship is distinct from all others that are established through violent means. If his own rule were a reign that could be established through violence, then Jesus' followers would have fought to prevent him from being handed over to his opponents. Yet the quality of Jesus' rule is such that it cannot be advanced through violent means.

Jesus' full reply does *not* indicate that his kingship is inconsequential for Roman kingship. On the contrary, this reply implies a certain tension between Jesus' kingship and those kingships that are established through violence. Fundamentally, Jesus does not seek to overthrow Roman kingship and to establish his own kingship by violent means. Nevertheless, his kingship, without violence, serves as a standard for measuring the Roman kingship premised upon violence. There are thus two major affirmations contained within Jesus' reply: (a) he does indeed possess kingship, and (b) his kingship, in contrast with Roman kingship, is not based upon violence.

John portrays Pilate as desirous of knowing more about the way in which Jesus is a king (18:37a). In his reply Jesus acknowledges again that he is indeed a king but insists on his own meaning of that term. He now refers to his preexistence and incarnation and stresses that his kingship is focused on bearing witness to the truth: "For this was I born, and for this I have come into the world, to bear witness to the truth" (18:37b).

Over the next verses of John's account, Jesus' adversaries remain intransigent despite Pilate's initiatives to have Jesus released. Increasingly frustrated and now uneasy, Pilate pointedly asks Jesus (19:9b): "Where are you from?" John states expressly that Jesus refused to answer this question and implies the stance of someone with superior standing not deigning to answer the query of someone lower. Pilate regards this response as outrageous given his own estimation of the Roman power he wields: "You will not speak to me? Do you not know that I have power to release you and power to crucify you?" (19:10).

At this stage John's portrayal of Jesus' sovereignty is particularly memorable. Jesus does not consider that he is dependent on Pilate for his life, and he is not intimidated by Pilate's brandishing of his power. The essential thrust of Jesus' reply is to testify to Pilate concerning the existence of a higher order. Far from negotiating with Pilate for his life, Jesus confronts the governor with the fact that he would have no power over him unless Jesus' betrayal had been permitted to occur in accordance with the Father's ordered plan. Because the nuances of the original Greek are somewhat difficult to capture in English, a phrase has been inserted in the translation of this important verse in order to clarify that Pilate is, in fact, located within a framework of events that is given from above. Jesus' pronouncement is as follows: "You would have no power over me unless it [this framework of events] had been given you from above; therefore he who delivered me to you has the greater sin" (19:11).

The Johannine Jesus' reflection that Pilate would have *no power* except for God's sovereign unfolding of events is immediately of interest. This assertion by Jesus represents a highly direct engagement with the question of Roman power. Significantly, the Greek text provides no basis for the frequent interpretation that power to rule has been duly given to Pilate by God. The text does not state that God has invested Pilate (or his Roman superiors) with sovereign power. Rather, Pilate is only allowed to exercise power over Jesus because there is a larger scenario of divinely ordered events in which Jesus' trial has a place.[2]

The two major pronouncements by the Johannine Jesus at the time of his Roman trial thus testify memorably to the sovereign kingship of Jesus and the surpassing ordering power of God. Taken together, they represent a coherent position regarding a circumscribed role for the Roman governor within the providence of God. Pilate, the Roman governor of Judea, is allowed in the ordering of God to decree Jesus' crucifixion. Yet ultimately it is Jesus who possesses full sovereignty. He is sovereign as a king whose rule is based not on violence but rather on bearing witness to the truth.

JESUS' PREDICTIONS REGARDING ROMAN PERSECUTION

Within the canonical text of John's Gospel there is one clear instance of Jesus predicting martyrdom at the hands of the Roman rulers and another instance in which his words may allude to a life-threatening reaction by the Roman authorities. In chapter 3 above it has been noted that in the Synoptic accounts, Jesus explicitly warns regarding persecutions by "governors and kings." In John's account a relatively greater emphasis is placed on the hostile reaction of the allied Sanhedrin parties. Nevertheless, in portraying Jesus' farewell address in chapter 16, John reports a warning that may allude to persecution by the Roman authorities. Later, in chapter 21, Jesus' words are evidently intended to warn Peter regarding his own Roman martyrdom.

It should be noted first, in regard to 16:2, that the first clause of this verse mentions persecution by the synagogue authorities. In the preceding verse, Jesus has mentioned that one of his purposes in discoursing with them is to strengthen them against falling away. It is in this context that he states (16:2a): "They will put you out of synagogues."

Jesus' next words may represent a continuation of this warning regarding actions by the Jewish authorities. However, it is also possible that these words extend his line of thought regarding persecution into another area, namely, into the area of persecution by the political authorities. Here is Jesus' next comment: "Indeed the hour is coming when whoever kills you will think he is offering service to God" (16:2b).

In the present interpretation, Jesus has finished speaking of persecution by the synagogue authorities and is referring to the phenomenon of persecution by the Roman authorities. His words now pertain to a situation in which the executions of Christians occur at the order of pagan rulers who are desirous of propitiating pagan gods. There are various considerations that argue in support of this interpretation, yet it is scarcely possible to resolve the issue decisively. That the emperor Trajan persecuted Christians for refusing to acknowledge the pagan gods he considered responsible for his victories over the Dacians and Scythians is but one of a number of factors that may bear upon this matter.

In contrast with the indeterminacy of 16:2 regarding the agents of persecution, it can be clearly established that in 21:18–19 the Roman authorities are envisioned as those who will be responsible for Peter's martyrdom. While there is an allusive quality about

Jesus' words in 21:18, the final author of the Gospel takes pains to clarify in 21:19 that death by crucifixion is meant:

> "Truly, truly, I say to you, when you were young, you girded yourself and walked where you would; but when you are old, you will stretch out your hands, and another will gird you and carry you where you do not wish to go." (This he said to show by what death he was to glorify God.) And after this he said to him, "Follow me." (21:18–19)

In 21:18, the images of Peter's arms stretched out from his body and of his being girded by another and carried where he does not wish to go all pertain to death by crucifixion. And 21:19 indicates that this form of death will be a means of glorifying God, just as earlier in the Gospel Jesus' death by crucifixion was simultaneously his glorification. In other words, having reconciled Peter and given him a remarkable pastoral commission in 21:15–17, the risen Jesus now indicates that Peter is called to follow his Lord in the specific manner of death by crucifixion. "Follow me" is indeed the directive with which 21:19 ends, a directive that is repeated and intensified in 21:22b.

It remains to note and then to emphasize that martyrdom through crucifixion is unalterably martyrdom at the hands of the Roman authorities. For just as capital sentences were the prerogative of Roman administrators, so was crucifixion the preferred method of execution for those who were not Roman citizens. Within the empire of Jesus' day, as well as at the time when the Gospel was published, there was no entity or authority with the power to crucify apart from the various imperial administrators. In effect, then, Jesus here makes a significant prediction that Peter's death will be identical with Jesus' own manner of death: crucifixion at the hands of the Roman authorities.[3]

John's Own Perspective Regarding Imperial Propaganda

As the author who presented the Gospel for circulation, John remains an intriguing figure. Others may have contributed to shaping this work, but John himself took the decisive steps of finalizing it and authorizing its circulation. Who was John? In what city or regions did he reside? Was he immersed in the life of a particular Christian community?

Only one factor is agreed upon, although not always reflected upon, in the various theories concerning John and his circumstances. It is the fundamental datum that John lived and wrote from somewhere within the boundaries of the Roman empire. From this basic insight it can be concluded that John himself, a person with literary gifts and accomplishments, possessed an abiding familiarity with the realities of Roman rule.

Are there any indications of John's own perspective on Roman rule given by the contents of the completed Gospel? Caution must always be observed in trying to scrutinize a Gospel for clues regarding its author's interests and purposes. Nevertheless, it is possible to argue that the text of the Gospel suggests John's concern to provide an alternative perspective for the readers of the Gospel who were barraged by imperial propaganda regarding the sovereignty of the Roman emperors. It is also probable that another of John's purposes was to strengthen any of his Christian readers who were faced with imperial persecution.

It is well to begin this investigation concerning John's own mentality with considerations regarding four of Jesus' titles within the Gospel. We recall that, at the time of his trial, Jesus accepted the title of "King." Three other titles, each pertaining to sovereign power, are also accorded to him and accepted by him within John's account: "Lord," "Savior of the World," and "Lord and God." Significantly, each of these titles was claimed by one or more of the first-century Roman emperors.

What is John's perspective regarding these titles? What does his inclusion of pericopes featuring these titles reveal concerning his own outlook? John's own author's notes (20:30–31; 21:25) disclose that he faced major decisions regarding selectivity: myriads of reports concerning Jesus might be included, but John worked within the self-imposed limit of a single scroll. The pericopes included in the final text are thus surely included because John accorded them a high priority.

In the Gospel of John, "Lord" (*kyrios*) is the preeminent title of address used by those who truly believe in Jesus. This pattern holds for the time of Jesus' public ministry and also characterizes the interval of his postresurrection appearances. In addition, after Jesus' resurrection, Mary Magdalene, the beloved disciple, and others use the term "*the* Lord" in speaking of Jesus objectively. Significantly, Mary also refers to Jesus as "*my* Lord" (20:13).

In addition to its use by Jesus' disciples, "Lord" is also used by a number of other persons within the Gospel who are in the process of coming to believe in Jesus. This is particularly true for those involved in situations in which Jesus heals. In addition, John, as narrator, occasionally uses "Lord" in reference to Jesus. Finally, when he washes his disciples' feet, Jesus himself explicitly utilizes this term in self-designation (13:13–14a).

From the standpoint of the present study, what is particularly significant in respect to many of these occurrences of "Lord" is that they serve unmistakably to convey and enhance the meaning that Jesus is a figure of exalted standing, someone whose sovereign power extends even to the limits of life and death. The narrative of Martha's and Mary's interactions with Jesus at the time of Lazarus' death provides a striking example of this unsurpassed sovereignty.

Initially, when Martha and Mary seek out Jesus, Lazarus is seriously ill. In contacting him they address him as "Lord" and their message also evidences their trust that Jesus has the power to restore Lazarus to health (11:3–4). By the time Jesus arrives on the scene, Lazarus had died. However, Martha (again addressing Jesus as "Lord") expresses trust that even now Jesus can intervene with power (11:21–22). In a beautiful exchange Jesus asserts that he has sovereign power over death and asks Martha if she believes this (11:23–26). In her response Martha wonderfully expresses her belief in Jesus' exalted, sovereign standing: "Yes, *Lord*; I believe that you are the Christ, the Son of God, he who is coming into the world" (11:27).

Before proceeding to the tomb, Jesus next meets with Mary, who like her sister, addresses him as "Lord" and replicates Martha's exact confession (11:32b). Arriving at the site, Jesus reassures Martha of his power to intervene and then prays aloud to the Father. Remarkably, he prays not in petition but rather for the purpose of indicating to those assembled his own close relationship with the Father (11:41b–42). Jesus, the one addressed and reverenced as "Lord" throughout this episode, then authoritatively and sovereignly bids Lazarus to come forth from the tomb (11:43–44).

Each of the other titles that reflect Jesus' unexcelled sovereignty occurs only once within John's Gospel. Nevertheless, in each instance, the title strikingly culminates a dramatic episode that John has narrated at length. It is as though John instinctively recognized the far-reaching implications of each title and desired to present each in a way that would allow it to have maximum impact.

The title "Savior of the World" is presented as the climax of Jesus' encounter with the Samaritans in chapter 4 of the Gospel. As is well known, this episode begins when Jesus initiates a conversation with a Samaritan woman by requesting a drink of water from her. The narrative then progresses through a series of stages in which the woman, in almost steplike fashion, comes to appreciate the various aspects of Jesus' identity.

When Jesus' disciples return, the woman departs and begins to proclaim Jesus to the inhabitants of her city. Moved by her testimony, the townspeople themselves begin to believe in Jesus and prevail upon him to remain with them. At the conclusion of his time with them, the townspeople speak decisively to the woman: "It is no longer because of your words that we believe, for we have heard for ourselves, and we know that this is indeed *the Savior of the world*" (4:42).

It is well to explicate two aspects of the powerful meaning that John has achieved in positioning this title as the memorable culmination of this episode. As used here this title extends *universally*. At the same time, this title is also used *exclusively*. The titles of "Prophet" and "Messiah" appear earlier in this episode and disclose aspects of Jesus' identity that are especially significant within a Jewish context. Both of these aspects are then taken up into a more universal frame of reference when Jesus is acclaimed as Savior . . . *of the World*. For John evidently understands that the Samaritans are not merely confessing that Jesus is the Savior of Samaritans and Jews. Rather, the saving work for which the Samaritans acclaim him extends beyond the territories of Judea and Galilee and Samaria and encompasses the entire world.

In order to appreciate that "Savior of the World," is here used *exclusively* of Jesus, attention needs to be given to the other passages in John's Gospel (for example 3:17 and 12:44) in which Jesus characterizes his mission as a "saving" of the world. For according to John's account, Jesus really does have the power to "save."

The present question is whether John understands the Samaritans to be proclaiming that Jesus *alone* is Savior of the World. In other words, does John present the Samaritans claiming that Jesus is the Savior of the World in a way that could never be rivaled by an emperor such as Nero or a pagan god of healing such as Asclepius? The presence of the word "indeed" (*alēthos*) in the Samaritans' proclamation is one sign that a decisive affirmation of Jesus as Savior is intended. In this reading the Samaritans are implicitly recognizing that others may style themselves as saviors, but Jesus is *indeed* the Savior of the World. Second, the studied, solemn character of the Samaritans' declaration *seems* also lends weight to the interpretation that their words mean that Jesus has no rival with respect to *real* power for saving the world.

Why did John prominently display this title as one so fittingly used of Jesus? Why did he portray Jesus in other passages of his Gospel as the one who truly accomplishes the saving of the world? The argument of the present study is that John did so to encourage his readers not ever to be swayed or intimidated by the aggrandizing claims of the Roman emperors who styled themselves as saviors. Certainly other factors may have influenced John to include these dramatic encounters in Samaria in his final account. Nevertheless, he surely intended to stress that no other figure or entity was comparable to Jesus.

In addition to repeated references to Jesus as "Lord" and a singular reference to him as "Savior of the World," John also includes Thomas' momentous acclamation of Jesus as "Lord and God." The inclusion of such a title anywhere in the Gospel would have immediately engaged the attention of readers who may have been familiar with the emperor Domitian's controversial appropriation of this title. In point of fact, John has placed the episode involving this title at the climax, the very finale of his account.

In his postresurrection appearances, Jesus is no longer subject to the constraints of space and time. He has the capacity to come into the midst of the disciples despite closed doors. He has the capacity to know the unbelief that Thomas expressed during the week between Jesus' two appearances. By reporting Thomas' failure in the way that he does, John engenders a sense of anticipation or apprehension regarding the resolution of the situation. What will Jesus say when he addresses Thomas? What will Thomas do when he encounters Jesus?

As the narrative unfolds, the first step was taken by the risen Jesus. Jesus invites Thomas to place his fingers at the crucifixion marks in Jesus' hands and to put his hand into the opening in Jesus' side made by the Roman soldier's spear. In doing so Thomas should no longer be unbelieving, but rather believing. To this invitation Thomas responds with the following worshipful words: "My Lord and my God!" (20:28).

Simply by positioning these words at the summit of the body of the Gospel, John ensured that they would inevitably command the attention of every reader and auditor. Yet, in this literary structuring, Thomas' acclamation also constitutes a magnificent closing echo for the sublime testimony that John himself had given to Jesus in his prologue. Indeed, in the very first verse of the Gospel, John stated that "the Word was with God and the Word was God." In John's literary structure, Thomas' acclamation of Jesus' majesty and divinity thus powerfully complements the Gospel's opening themes in a way that is particularly significant in the context of the imperial ruler cult.

The fact that Thomas' acclamation expresses his intense personal allegiance to Jesus as Lord and God should also be noted. On the one hand, the unadorned words "Lord and God" acknowledge that Jesus is, objectively, the Lord and God of the universe. On the other hand, the presence of the personal adjective "my" indicates Thomas' intense sense of being in relationship with Jesus. In the previous verses, Jesus was intensely *"my* Lord" for Mary Magdalene. Now he is intensely *"my* Lord and *my* God" for Thomas. Again, within a Roman context in which allegiance is being sought for the person of the emperor, Thomas' manifestation of a deeply personal allegiance to Jesus takes on added meaning.

In this dramatic finale to the body of John's Gospel, Jesus' status as Lord and God is not limited or circumscribed. Thomas' words and the entire scene that John is portraying allow for the risen

Jesus' continuing presence. Jesus is not Lord and God for one week or for one year. Nor shall there be any limit to Thomas' allegiance to him. For just as Jesus is unendingly Lord and God, so must Thomas' confession of him be unending.

In summary, the argument of this section up to this point is that John intended to emphasize Jesus' sovereignty in the face of the aggressive efforts by the Roman emperors and their attendants to appropriate such titles as "Lord," "Savior of the World," and "Lord and God." John may also have intended to respond to Roman peace propaganda by emphasizing Jesus' role as the author of true peace. As noted above, in 18:36 Jesus responded to Pilate that his servants would fight for him if his kingship were "of the world." Nevertheless, Jesus' rule was to be furthered not by violence but rather by bearing witness to the truth. Jesus' explicit words regarding the character of his peace were spoken at the final supper: "Peace I leave with you; my peace I give to you; not as the world gives do I give to you. Let not your hearts be troubled, neither let them be afraid" (14:27). When these words are correlated with Jesus' words to Pilate, they constitute a magisterial reply to imperial claims regarding the "peace" conferred by Augustus and his successors. Like the Roman emperors, Jesus claims to confer peace and its related benefits. However, the Roman peace is imposed by means of violence and is "of this world." Jesus' peace, in contrast, can never be furthered by violent means.

JOHN'S GOSPEL AND ROMAN PERSECUTION

In addition to his desire to encourage his readers to reject the claims associated with the imperial ruler cult, John arguably had another purpose in writing—to strengthen and encourage any of his readers who were facing Roman persecution or the threat of such persecution. It is clear from the famous letter of Pliny, the Roman governor of Pontus-Bithynia, to the emperor Trajan that Pliny was engaged in persecuting Christians within that province.[4] This letter was written circa A.D. 110, but in it Pliny refers to earlier trials involving Christians and implies that Trajan himself has some familiarity with what has transpired. There is a distinct possibility that the earlier trials to which Pliny refers occurred during the regime of Domitian (81–96). However, the only datable Roman persecution of Christians during the first century was that carried out by Nero in A.D. 64.

Apart from the persecutions that occurred under Pliny and Nero, the phenomenon of official Roman persecution of Christians in the first century is difficult to confirm in the surviving historical sources. Nevertheless, even if there were only these instances of officially sanctioned persecution (see chapter 6 below for a discussion of the unofficial forms of persecution faced by Christians in Asia Minor), it is still possible that John intended to strengthen his readers against any looming Roman persecution.

Fundamentally such an argument focuses on Jesus' disclosure to his disciples that they would face persecution and his specific prediction that Peter would face crucifixion. In a similar vein, John may have provided a lengthy description of Jesus' conduct before Pilate out of a concern to provide Christians with a model in case they themselves were arraigned by Roman governors. Finally, the extended attention that John devotes to several important concepts in Jesus' farewell discourses may also reflect the evangelist's concern to strengthen Christians for facing persecution. The concept of the Holy Spirit as the disciples' Paraclete, that is, as their *trial attorney,* is particularly relevant in this regard.

In summary, the author of John's Gospel lived under Roman rule, was well familiar with its realities, and had, as one of his purposes, the strengthening of Christians who were themselves immersed in the currents and controversies of Roman rule. For these disciples, John memorably communicated Jesus' teachings regarding Roman power, Jesus' proclamation regarding the nature of his own kingship, and Jesus' warnings relative to future persecution. For these later disciples, John also provided a series of reports concerning the ways in which Jesus' first followers had acclaimed his unexcelled sovereignty and expressed their own commitment to him.

To conceptualize vividly what John achieved for the disciples of his own day, it is useful to imagine these disciples with copies of

John's Gospel at hand as they gathered for a communal discernment of their own priorities in the face of imperial propaganda and in the face of other imperial demands and threats.

Notes

1. The analysis of this chapter fundamentally follows R. Cassidy, *John's Gospel in New Perspective: Christology and the Realities of Roman Power* (Maryknoll, N.Y.: Orbis Books, 1992).

2. It is thus *a significant misinterpretation* to assert that the meaning of John 19:11 is in alignment with the meaning of Roman 13:1–7.

3. See pp. 89–95 below for the interpretation that Paul, in Philippians, came to recognize that he might well suffer much the same form of death (execution by decree of the Roman authorities) as Jesus his Lord suffered. See Philippians 3:10b: ". . . becoming like him in his death." Chapter 9 below will advance the thesis that the early Christian communities who read the texts of the New Testament found ample references to persecution and martyrdom at the hands of the Roman authorities.

4. For the texts of Pliny's letter and Trajan's rescript, see Cassidy, *John's Gospel in New Perspective,* 89–91; for analysis of these documents, see ibid., 17–26.

5

The Acts of the Apostles
and Roman Rule

U P TO THIS POINT, the focus has been upon Jesus' responses
to Roman rule according to the Synoptic Gospels and
according to the Gospel of John. Except for comments
regarding the personal perspectives of Luke and John, little attention has been given to the perspective and conduct of Jesus' disciples with respect to Roman power. Accordingly, this chapter and
those following will treat the response of several of Jesus' leading
disciples: Peter, John, and especially Paul.

The present chapter will examine Luke's portrayal of Jesus' followers in the Acts of the Apostles.[1] The first section will present a
brief overview of the phenomenon of Roman rule within Acts.
Section two will analyze the response to Roman rule that Luke
attributes to the leading members of the Jerusalem community.
Sections three and four will be devoted to an analysis of Luke's
reports concerning Paul. The demarcation between these latter two
sections is provided by Claudius Lysias' arrest and chaining of Paul.

SALIENT FEATURES OF ROMAN RULE
IN ACTS

Acts is so filled with references to Roman rule that justice can
scarcely be done to all of them within a single chapter section.

51

Nevertheless, the paragraphs that follow will provide a cursory treatment of Luke's references to the particularities of Roman rule in Judea and in Rome's other eastern provinces. The capital of the empire, Rome itself, will also be viewed through the lens of Acts.

As regards Roman rule in Judea, the fact that the Roman authorities' decision to allow the Sanhedrin in Jerusalem to exercise substantive power is of critical importance for the narrative of Acts just as it was for the narrative of the Gospel. Acts portrays this council as dominated by the chief priests of the Sadducean party but with an admixture of Pharisees as well. A significant part of the conflict of Acts derives from the implacable hostility of the chief priests to the memory of Jesus and any proclamations about him. Paul initially was allied with the chief priestly group, but came to be viewed as a traitor to their cause as a result of his startling conversion to Jesus.

Other features of Roman rule in Judea that are important for Acts are the identities and offices of the various Roman administrators with whom the chief priests were associated. In Acts 12, Herod Agrippa I (a grandson of Herod the Great, he had been appointed as king by Gaius and confirmed by Claudius) martyred James and imprisoned Peter. Claudius Lysias, the tribune of the Roman forces stationed in Jerusalem was the officer who arrested and chained Paul, subsequently sending him to Antonius Felix at the Roman governor's headquarters at Caesarea on the Mediterranean coast (Acts 21–24). Two years later Porcius Festus replaced Felix as governor and inherited Paul's case. According to Acts 25, Herod Agrippa II (the son of Herod Agrippa I) paid a visit to Caesarea and played a role in advising Festus regarding the appeal to Caesar that Paul had made.

As distinct from Judea, which, as an imperial province, was directly subject to the emperor, Macedonia, Achaia, and Asia were senatorial provinces governed (normally) by senators who had previously served as consuls. Paul was in jeopardy in each of these provinces, but it was only at Corinth in Achaia that his case was heard by the highest authority, the proconsul himself. At Philippi, "magistrates" were directly involved in arresting and imprisoning Paul. In Thessalonica, the rioting crowds appealed to the "politarchs" against Paul. In Ephesus, the "city manager" was the person responsible for quelling the riot and determining that complaints against Paul would be settled in the regular assembly. Below more will be said about each of these upper-echelon Roman authorities. The point presently being made is that Acts reflects that various types of local governing arrangements were possible within the overall scheme of Roman political administration.

In Acts, Rome, the capital of the empire, emerges as the geographical goal to which the narrative is heading from 19:21 onward. Visible manifestations of Roman power dot the pages of Acts, but there are virtually no references to the internal power configurations at Rome itself. Paul's mission to proclaim the Gospel authoritatively in Rome is anticipated by the risen Jesus' mandate: "you shall be my witnesses in Jerusalem and in all Judea and Samaria and to the ends of the earth" (1:8b). Imperial roads, well marked with milestones, emanated from the hub of Rome to the farthest reaches of the empire. For the Gospel to be preached authoritatively at the center of Rome meant that, in principle, it was on its way to the farthest reaches of the world.

A second way in which the imperial capital is vitally present with Acts is as the seat of Caesar's tribunal. According to Luke's report, Paul had already been kept in chains for two years when Porcius Festus, the new governor, proposed a shift in venue that would have placed Paul in great jeopardy. Outraged by this proposal, Paul boldly appealed to have his case heard personally by Caesar (25:11). From that time forward Paul is propelled toward Rome, not as a free apostle but rather as a chained prisoner seeking vindication at the emperor's tribunal. And thus, in Acts, Rome is both a key geographical situs for the authoritative proclamation of the Gospel and the supreme judicial site at which a just verdict may (possibly) be rendered.

THE POLITICAL STANCE
OF THE JERUSALEM COMMUNITY

In the opening chapters of Acts, descriptions pertaining to the social stance and the political stance of the Jerusalem community are intertwined. Several of the episodes that Luke narrates can be grouped in terms of public testimony about Jesus by the apostles and disciples and the efforts of the chief priests and their allies to dissuade and punish them for giving such testimony.

In Acts 7, as a result of his uncompromising testimony before the Sanhedrin, Stephen becomes the first disciple to suffer martyrdom. From the character of Luke's descriptions, it is not clear whether he considers Stephen's execution to be the product of "lynch law" or whether he understands the Sanhedrin to be exercising a special prerogative for issuing and carrying out a death sentence. In either case, what is clear is that the Sanhedrin's role in Stephen's death is decisive.

In the two encounters that Peter, John, and the other apostles have with the Sanhedrin, the outcome is not as deadly. Nevertheless the stance of unshakable loyalty to the risen Jesus that was manifested by Stephen is also the same fundamental stance that is twice manifested by the apostles. It is instructive to consider the declarations made by Peter and John after they had initially been ordered not to speak or teach in the name of Jesus. Subsequently Peter and the other apostles were rearrested for failing to heed this directive. And during Peter's second appearance before the Sanhedrin, he and the others again boldly indicated that they would persevere in their testimony on behalf of Jesus. These responses to the Sanhedrin are as follows:

> Whether it is right in the sight of God to listen to you rather than to God, you must judge: for we cannot but speak of what we have seen and heard. (4:19–20)

> But Peter and the apostles answered, "We must obey God rather than men. The God of our fathers raised Jesus whom you killed by hanging him on a tree. God exalted him at his right hand as Leader and Savior, to give repentance to Israel and forgiveness of sins. And we are witnesses to these things, and so is the Holy Spirit whom God has given to those who obey him." (5:29–32)

Significantly, in both instances, the apostles do not question the Sanhedrin's authority for ordering them them to desist from public preaching in Jerusalem. No argument is made that the Sanhedrin has exceeded its authority in trying to prohibit this activity. Rather, while seeming to recognize the Sanhedrin's role in overseeing public order, the apostles nevertheless refuse to obey the council's directives in this matter.

Second, in both replies, but especially in their second reply, the apostles justify their disobedience to the Sanhedrin by avowing their obedience to God. In effect, they claim that the Sanhedrin's directives are not in accordance with God's purposes. And given this disparity, given a situation in which there is irreconcilable disparity between the Sanhedrin's decree and God's desires, the apostles must necessarily further the objectives of God.

The open-ended character of both of these responses should be underscored. In the concrete circumstances of the Acts narrative, the Jerusalem Sanhedrin is the religiopolitical entity whose directives are set aside for lack of conformity with God's purposes. Yet the principle enunciated by the apostles in both instances is not limited in its implications to the decrees of the Sanhedrin. A close literal translation of the apostles' declaration in 5:29 would be: "It is necessary to obey God rather than human beings." If there were to be conflicts between the purposes of God and the decrees of a Herodian king, of a Roman governor, or even of the emperor himself, it is evident that such a principled declaration commits the disciples of Jesus to full-hearted obedience to the desires of God.

Finally, the congruence between these two principled declarations and the teaching of the Jesus in the Synoptic Gospels about rendering to Caesar the things that are Caesar's and to God the things that are God's should not be overlooked. In effect, Luke's Jesus (and the Jesus of Mark and Matthew) expostulates that the things of God are the criteria against which the things of Caesar are to be evaluated. Transposing this teaching into the present context, it can be said that the leaders of the Jerusalem church have decided that the Sanhedrin's directives do not reflect "the things of God." Given this lack of conformity with God's purposes, the directives of this council do not merit the apostles' compliance.[2]

According to Luke's narrative, the apostles' second bold declaration enraged the Sanhedrin members to such a degree that they wanted to kill them. Nevertheless, the Pharisee Gamaliel's intervention proved persuasive and the apostles were given a beating and dismissed under a new order not to proclaim Jesus, an order that they promptly violated (5:33–42).

As noted previously, the Sanhedrin subsequently initiated action that resulted in Stephen's martyrdom. Somewhat later, after the conversion of Paul and after the decisive opening of the mission to the Gentiles that was effected by Peter's baptism of Cornelius, Luke indicates that new measures against the disciples were initiated by Herod Agrippa I. These measures were seemingly at the behest of the chief priests and their allies on the Sanhedrin. In laying "violent hands" upon some members of the Jerusalem church, Herod killed the apostle James "with the sword." He then arrested and jailed Peter with a view to executing him only to have this plan thwarted through divine intervention (12:1–11).

It is thus the case that, by chapter 12 of Acts, the following events have ensued: (a) Peter and John arrested and threatened; (b) the apostles as a group imprisoned, beaten, and threatened; (c) Stephen martyred; (d) James the apostle executed; (e) Peter arrested with a view to execution. In the first three instances, the Sanhedrin is clearly the threatening entity. In the latter two, it is Herod Agrippa I. His execution of James with the sword may imply a judgment of disloyal or treasonous conduct. At any event, just as Jesus their Lord was executed by the decree of a Roman governor, so now is James executed through the decree of a Roman king.

Before closing this analysis of the controversies involving Jesus' disciples and the Sanhedrin and the apostles and Herod Agrippa I, attention should be focused upon the Greek word *parrhēsia* as Luke's preferred term for describing the disciples' conduct and testimony throughout this section. The primary meaning of the term is "boldness," especially boldness in political and ethical contexts. It will be explained below that boldness is the defining characteristic of Paul's testimony in Rome and that Luke highlights this quality in the sentence with which he ends the narrative of Acts. In the present context Luke uses "boldness" to characterize Peter's speech at Pentecost and to describe the conduct of Peter and John at their first Sanhedrin arraignment.

Significantly, after they had been solemnly admonished and dismissed by the Sanhedrin, Peter and John gathered with the other members of the church and prayed for the needed strength not to be intimidated by the rulers. Their prayers culminated in this petition (4:29): "And now, Lord, look upon their threats and grant to thy servants to speak thy word *with all boldness."* Luke then reports (4:30): "And when they had prayed, the place in which they were gathered together was shaken; and they were all filled with the Holy Spirit and spoke the word of God *with boldness."*

PAUL'S CONTROVERSIES PRIOR TO HIS ARREST AND CHAINING

It has sometimes been said that the Acts of the Apostles might appropriately have been titled "The Acts of Paul." Although exaggerated, such a statement serves to focus attention on the significant role that Paul plays within Luke's overall narrative. Luke includes three distinct reports concerning Paul's conversion and he writes at considerable length concerning Paul's missionary activity on behalf of Jews and Gentiles alike. A further dimension of Luke's treatment of Paul, a dimension that is often insufficiently appreciated, is Luke's portrayal of Paul as an apostle who engendered controversies in four Roman provinces. Another frequently neglected aspect of Luke's narrative is his portrayal of Paul as a chained Roman prisoner authorized to proclaim Jesus his Lord in the capital of the empire.

The present section examines the nature of Paul's controversies and the nature of his interactions with various Roman officials prior to his arrest in Jerusalem as well as Paul's Roman citizenship. At the outset of this investigation of Paul's experiences in Philippi, Thessalonica, Corinth, and Ephesus, it is worth noting that Luke repeatedly narrates episodes in which Paul comes into conflict with various Roman authorities. To be sure, Luke also portrays Paul's conflicts with Jews who refuse to accept his message. Luke further details Paul's conflicts with Christians who advocate the observance of the Jewish law. Still, to a remarkable degree, Luke's narrative concentrates on conflicts that lead to the involvement of the Roman authorities.

There is nothing in these descriptions to suggest that Paul intentionally disrupted the Roman order. In Luke's portrayal, Paul is by no means "anti-Roman." Nevertheless, in the situations that Luke describes Paul is frequently a de facto disturber of the Roman peace. Time after time, his preaching of Jesus and his uncompromising allegiance to Jesus as his Lord result in upheaval, tumult, and the involvement of the Roman authorities.

Paul's visit to Philippi in Acts 16 serves as an apt illustration for many of the preceding observations. This passage also contains Paul's first reference to his Roman citizenship. In the course of his ministry in this highly Roman city (founded as a "colony" of Roman veterans, Philippi was principally composed of Roman citizens and was Roman in its customs), Paul expelled a demonic spirit from a possessed girl whose masters were exploiting her clairvoyance. Ironically (because Paul and Silas are themselves Roman citizens), her outraged masters denounce Paul for "disturbing our city" and state that Paul and Silas "advocate customs which it is not lawful for us Romans to accept or practice" (16:20–21).

Faced with this charge, the Roman authorities of Philippi, "the magistrates," are then shown to behave in a totally inappropriate fashion. Without any serious investigation into the situation, the magistrates themselves pull the garments off the two apostles, order them to be severely beaten, and then throw them into prison. Wondrous events in support of Paul (including an earthquake) subsequently ensue and, seemingly, one effect is to bring about a change of heart in the magistrates. Paul nevertheless refuses an offer of release on the grounds that the magistrates have grievously violated their rights as Roman citizens. The outcome is that the magistrates must come and "conciliate" with them before Paul and Silas will agree to leave.

In addition to Paul's standing as a zealous Jew, a committed Christian, and a citizen of Tarsus, Luke has now shown that Paul possesses Roman citizenship. Why has this significant datum not been mentioned by Luke until now? In Luke's account, Paul was willing to accept a beating rather than publicly trumpet his citizenship. Below it will be observed how Paul follows a comparable course in Jerusalem. In public settings Paul thus manifests a certain "reserve" or "reluctance" about his citizenship. However, in private confrontations with Roman officials who have violated his rights, Paul three times adverts to his prerogatives as a citizen.[3]

In Philippi, Gentiles formulated the charges against Paul and no

Jews played a role. In Thessalonica in Acts 17, the principal insti-
gators against Paul were Jews who rejected his teaching. Unable to
locate Paul, they denounced Jason and some of Paul's other converts to the politarchs. Although formulated by Jews, the charges
against Paul at Thessalonica are similar to those at Philippi:
"These men who have turned the world upside down have come
here also, and Jason has received them; and they are all acting
against the decrees of Caesar, saying that there is another king,
Jesus" (17:6–7).

Briefly, two facets of these charges should be noted. The first
facet is that Paul is alleged to disturb the Roman order. The second
facet is that Paul is doing so because of his allegiance to a king
other than Caesar. These charges are made in bad faith but have
"the color of truth" about them. Paul's primary allegiance is to
Jesus, and he is preaching vigorously on behalf of Jesus. In Luke's
perspective, it is false to state that Paul is intentionally striving to
disrupt the Roman order in Thessalonica. Nevertheless, in Luke's
portrayal, the consequence of Paul's vigorous ministry is that the
"order" of the city is actually disrupted.

After Jason and others post bond for him, Paul continues his
missionary journey to Beroea, Athens, and Corinth. Paul's conduct
of his ministry for a year and a half in Corinth, the provincial capital, brought many of the Jews of the city to believe in Jesus. However, this result provoked a harsh reaction by those Jews who were
not persuaded. Paul was once again denounced to the highest
Roman authority in the province. In this instance the denunciation was to the proconsul Gallio, and Paul was apparently charged
with violating Jewish and Roman law (18:13). In Luke's description
of the outcome, Paul was spared in a surprising way. Gallio did not
exonerate Paul from the charges. Rather, evidencing his own anti-
Semitism, he peremptorily dismissed the case without even inves-
tigating the charges! In this remarkable outworking of God's
providence, Paul thus remained free for additional public ministry
on Jesus' behalf.

Several episodes intervene between the controversy in Corinth
and the public controversy in Ephesus that Luke describes in Acts
19. In the controversy in Ephesus, those instigating against Paul
were Gentiles offended that Paul's preaching had diminished the

cult of Artemis. Luke reports that Demetrius and his allies engendered widespread turbulence and describes a pandemonic assembly in the theater. Paul meanwhile was counseled by his friends not to try to enter the theater.

Once again, nothing in Luke's reports suggests that Paul consciously provoked this controversy. Nevertheless controversy was indeed occasioned by Paul's vigorous preaching. In this instance, the city manager of Ephesus, whose authority is subservient to that of the proconsul, exercised great discretion in quelling the riot. Because of this Roman official's adroit handling of the situation, Paul was able to journey back to Greece and then to undertake his final journey to Jerusalem.

It is at this stage of Luke's narrative that the first reference to the chains that await Paul in Jerusalem is made. In his speech to the elders at Miletus, Paul discloses to them a word of the Holy Spirit that "chains and affliction" await Paul in Jerusalem (21:23). When Paul subsequently reaches Caesarea, this prophecy is communicated even more vividly by Agabus, who symbolically binds his feet with Paul's girdle stating (21:11): "So shall the Jews at Jerusalem bind the man who own this girdle and deliver him into the hands of the Gentiles." Paul's response is to re-affirm his resoluteness on Christ's behalf (20:13): "For I am ready not only to be chained but even to die at Jerusalem for the name of the Lord Jesus."

After Paul arrived in Jerusalem, the skeletal predictions made by Agabus and Paul were concretized and fulfilled in a remarkable sequence of events. When the riot instigated by some hostile Jews from Asia threw the city into tumult and endangered Paul's life, the Roman tribune rushed upon the scene and temporarily halted the riot by arresting Paul. The Roman soldiers then shackled Paul, probably binding him to a soldier on either side of him. Luke's report concerning this development is as follows: "Then the tribune came up and arrested him and ordered him to be bound with two chains" (21:33a).

Paul's subsequent experience as a chained prisoner will be analyzed in the next section of this study. The final issue to be treated here concerns Paul's Roman citizenship. When he was initially arrested as the riot raged about him, Paul surprised the tribune by speaking to him in Greek. In response to Lysias' next question about his identity, Paul stated only: "I am a Jew, from Tarsus in Cilicia, a citizen of no mean city" (21:39a). Later, however, in the confines of the Roman barracks, when he was on the verge of being whipped, Paul disclosed his Roman citizenship.

In effect, the sequence leading to this disclosure is consistent with what Luke has earlier portrayed occurring at Philippi. Paul does not reveal his citizenship in either public setting even though it is manifestly in his interest to do so. Only when he is secluded with Roman officials and their delegates does he display this aspect of his identity. In his subsequent conversation with Lysias, Paul comments that his citizenship came to him from birth (22:28). When the nuances of the conversation that Luke reports are carefully considered, Paul's meaning seems to be that Roman citizenship is not something that he has coveted, sought, or paid a price for in the manner of Lysias. Paul's citizenship was automatically accorded to him; he has not quested to achieve it.

PAUL AS A CHAINED PRISONER FROM CAESAREA TO ROME

The references to Paul's chains that are interspersed throughout the later chapters of Acts reveal a frequently neglected aspect of the *Paulusbild* of Acts. Within these chapters, it is actually the exception when Luke images Paul without his chains. And within Luke's time frame, Paul wears these chains for more than four years.

Luke indicates expressly that, when Lysias determined to bring Paul before the Jerusalem Sanhedrin, he ordered Paul's chains removed (22:30). An implication to be grasped here is that Lysias' discovery of Paul's citizenship (which had just been made) did not prevent him from keeping Paul in chains. In the aftermath of this tumultuous session, Paul's nephew learned of an assassination pact and informed Lysias, who responded by quickly remitting Paul under armed guard to the governor's residence in Caesarea. Since Paul was sent to Antonius Felix *as a prisoner*, Luke presumably understands that Paul was bound with chains during the journey to Caesarea.

Felix's command that Paul be imprisoned at Herod's praetorium is reported in 23:35b, but Luke does not explicitly indicate the conditions of Paul's custody. In 24:23 Felix orders an easing of the severity of Paul's situation but Luke does not state what this relaxation entailed with respect to Paul's guards or his chains. Does Luke understand that Paul was allowed to move about the praetorium more freely? Does he understand the directive to mean that Paul continued to wear chains, but was not as closely supervised by those who guarded him? Luke does point to one specific consequence of Felix's command: Paul's friends are now allowed to provide for his needs.

Luke's readers can only conjecture as to the kinds of service that Paul's friends were now able to render to him. The identity of these friends is also left to the reader's conjecture. In summary, what these very general descriptions seem to imply is that Paul was being held under a type of "military custody" (*custodia militaris*). As Luke's narrative progresses, it also emerges that, in Luke's eyes, Paul was all along bound, in some fashion, with chains.

In 24:27 Luke reports that, when Felix was replaced as governor by Porcius Festus two years later, Felix "left Paul in chains." Luke attributes this decision to the fact that Felix was anxious to curry favor with Paul's adversaries. This development, along with Luke's report in 24:26 that Felix hoped to receive a bribe from Paul can prove to be jarring for Luke's readers. For, in his initial depiction of this Roman governor, Luke reported that Felix had a rather accurate knowledge of "the Way" and that Felix frequently invited Paul to speak to him regarding faith in Jesus and regarding "justice and self-control and future judgment" (24:24–25). Nevertheless, jarring or not, Luke's description of this Roman governor must be summarized as follows: *seemingly* evenhanded as regards Paul's case at the outset, Felix proved to be venal and corrupt at the end of his appointment.

Luke's narrative of Paul's experiences under the new governor, Porcius Festus, provides crucial support for the interpretation that Paul has been kept in chains for the two years he was in custody in Caesarea. At the stunning culmination of his "defense" speech before the dignitaries that Festus assembled, Paul used his physical chains to appeal personally to Herod Agrippa II and his entire audience: "Whether short or long, I would to God that not only you but also all who hear me this day might become such as I am— *except for these chains*" (26:29).

In this scene, Paul is imaged in chains in a situation in which he poses no threat whatsoever. (The assembly consists of the Roman governor's invited guests). However, Luke's sense is not that Paul wore his chains only for ceremonial occasions. Luke rather understands these chains as a constant feature in Paul's life while he remained in Roman custody. Paul resents his chains not simply because he was wearing them at the time of his speech, but rather because he has been wearing them for more than two years! It was not Porcius Festus who introduced Paul into chains. Rather, in Luke's view, Paul has usually been in chains since the time that Lysias first bound him with them.

When Paul reaches Rome after surviving shipwreck, the normal circumstances of custody, replete with chains, resume. In some respects the form of custody described resembles what might be characterized in contemporary terms as "house arrest." Paul was not imprisoned in the public jail, the *carcer*, but rather at a location where he could easily receive welcome visitors.

How are the foregoing assertions to be documented? Very simply, by appealing to Luke's reports at the conclusion of Acts. Luke indicates in 28:16b that a soldier was assigned to guard Paul. He subsequently presents Paul himself making a dramatic reference to his physical chain in testifying to Jesus before a group of Jewish visitors. Eschewing any embarrassment at having to meet with them as a chained prisoner, Paul states memorably to the visiting delegation that "it is because of the hope of Israel that *I am bound with this chain*" (28:20b).

Before returning to the topic of Luke's portrayal of Paul as a prisoner in Rome at the end of Acts, there are additional aspects of Luke's portrayal of Paul's interactions with Festus that must be considered. A first aspect is that Festus (like Felix before him) ultimately entered into collusion with Paul's adversaries. For, despite his subsequent efforts to "reinterpret" his misconduct for Herod Agrippa II (25:14–22, esp. vv. 20–21), it is plain from Luke's narrative that Festus sought to do Paul's enemies "a favor" in seeking to transfer the prisoner's case back to Jerusalem (25:9).

A second aspect pertains to the issue of Paul's objectives when Luke portrays him invoking his status as a Roman citizen in order to appeal to Caesar. Paul's immediate objective is to prevent his transfer, and he admonishes Festus in strongly accusatory language (25:10–11). Paul does not merely rest content with this denunciation, however. He determines to take the matter out of Festus' hands by appealing to the emperor. In order to have his case removed from Festus' jurisdiction, Paul invokes his rights as a citizen. Nevertheless, there is nothing in Luke's report of this appeal that intimates any positive hope by Paul for receiving better treatment at the emperor's tribunal. His appeal to Caesar is a defensive measure that is forced upon him because of the malfeasance of two provincial governors.

The third important aspect regarding Paul's involvement with Festus centers on the tension between Festus' (lower case) *lord* and Paul's (upper case) *Lord.* For as a part of his strategy for involving Herod Agrippa II in the proceedings, Festus makes reference to the report that he will have to submit to the emperor, stating: "But I have nothing to write to *my lord* about him" (25:26). With the emperor thus explicitly designated as Festus' "lord," Luke's narrative thus opens the way to far-reaching reflections about the nature of Festus' allegiances in comparison with Paul's.

These reflections can be briefly summarized as follows. Festus' fundamental allegiance is accorded to the emperor in Rome, the sovereign who has appointed him as governor for Judea. To Paul's "Lord," Festus manifests no allegiance whatsoever. For Paul, in contrast, absolute allegiance is given to Jesus, the "Lord" who is everything to him. But what is the nature of Paul's allegiance to Festus' "lord"? What is the nature of Paul's allegiance to the emperor? These are now questions for consideration.

Ironically, the charges that were preferred against Paul in Thessalonica (17:6–7) reverberate here. Paul is, in fact, fundamentally loyal to "another king, Jesus." But is he disloyal to Festus' lord? It has been argued above that Paul, in Acts, is by no means anti-Roman in his approach. Nevertheless, Paul's allegiance to Jesus is the arbiter of his loyalty to every other entity. Significantly, Jesus is not simply someone whose memory Paul honors. Rather, he is for Paul a *living* Lord. Finally, in the pages of Acts, Paul *must* testify publicly to his Lord. Jesus is not merely someone whom Paul treasures and acclaims in private devotion.

The following situation obtains when Paul arrives in Rome in Acts 28: (a) Paul arrives at the center of the empire, where Caesar's lordship is palpable; (b) he arrives as a chained prisoner on appeal to the emperor; and (c) he arrives as a disciple whose commitment to proclaim Jesus as Lord is steadfast and unshakable. What then does Luke report regarding the course of Paul's ministry in Rome?

Two central features of Paul's circumstances in Rome have already been noted, that is, that he was guarded by a Roman soldier and that he was chained in some way. An additional feature that should now be noted is the fact that Paul apparently has some financial responsibility for the quarters where he was confined. Finally, it is extremely significant that Paul's custody in Rome endured for two whole years (and is not yet resolved as Luke closes his narrative).

This last point is explicitly reported by Luke in 28:30. It is a point that deserves to be underscored for the *Paulusbild* of Acts. For, in effect, Luke presents Paul as a chained Roman prisoner for two years in Caesarea and as a chained Roman prisoner for two years in Rome. This significant feature of Luke's portrait of Paul has frequently been underestimated.[4]

Upon reflection, an element of Paul's situation in Rome that is somewhat surprising by reason of its absence is the element of Paul being ministered to by a circle of friends. As noted, Luke portrayed Paul being supported in this way while he was in custody at Caesarea. Arguments from silence are notoriously fragile; nevertheless, Luke does not show the Christian community of Rome rallying around Paul during the two years he was in their midst as a prisoner. (Note that in 28:15 a delegation of Christians initially came out of the city to meet the arriving prisoner at the Forum of Appius.) To be sure, the focus of Luke's final paragraphs is Paul's personal faithfulness and his specific overtures to the leaders of the Jewish community in Rome. Nevertheless, the absence of any specific mention of Christian supporters (apart from the implied presence of Luke) raises the question of whether Luke intends his discerning readers to appreciate that Paul was somewhat isolated from the Christian community of Rome during the time of his custody there.

In indicating the hardships that Paul had endured in Rome (the limitations of his freedom, the phenomenon of his chains, etc.), what Luke surely intends to stress is that Paul has not been defeated by them. His spirit was not broken by anything he had experienced during his four plus years as a Roman prisoner. And just as he testified faithfully despite malfeasance by two Roman governors, Paul will presumably conduct himself with this same faithfulness when he is eventually brought to testify before the emperor.[5]

A careful interpretation of Acts 28:31, especially its final four words, is decisive for a correct understanding of Luke's image of Paul as the curtain of Acts draws to a close. Paul is spotlighted at center stage—in chains! He is at the center of an empire whose emperor desires to be known as "lord." Nevertheless, taking advantage of whatever possibilities he has with any who approach him, Paul faithfully preaches the kingdom of God and teaches regarding Jesus Christ, who alone is truly "the Lord." In Luke's own final words, Paul does this: *"with all boldness . . . indomitable."*

NOTES

1. Undergirding the exegesis and the reflections presented in this chapter is the analysis made in R. Cassidy, *Society and Politics in the Acts of the Apostles* (Maryknoll, N.Y.: Orbis Books, 1983).

2. Acts thus shows the disciples of Jesus practicing the "evaluative" approach that the Gospels attribute to Jesus. Below in chapter 9 it will be argued that this approach represents the principal legacy that the New Testament writers have bequeathed to Christians living in the third millennium.

In this instance, Jesus' disciples evaluate a political directive negatively and refuse to comply with it. However, this need not inevitably be the case any more than it would be the case for every political directive to be accepted and complied with. What is crucial is that every political program, policy, directive, and so on be evaluated from the perspective of "the things of God."

3. In addition to this passage concerning Philippi, see 22:25–29 in Jerusalem and Paul's appeal to Caesar (which seemingly presumes his

standing as a citizen) in 25:9–12. Following W. Stegemann and others, C. Roetzel challenges Luke's reliability on the matter of Paul's citizenship (*Paul: The Man and the Myth* [Minneapolis: Fortress, 1999], 21–22). Significantly, this criticism of Luke is vitiated by Roetzel's uncritical acceptance of the "political apologetic" theory (p. 21) regarding Luke's purposes in writing.

A further important facet is that Paul's reluctance regarding his citizenship in Acts actually comports well with the fact that he does not explicitly refer to this credential anywhere in his letters. Paul, traveling as an apostle and ambassador of Christ has no desire to complicate the reception of his preaching by "arriving under Roman colors" so to speak. In Acts, as noted above, Paul only announces his citizenship when he is being egregiously mistreated by Roman officials and even then he does so only in "private" settings. The absence of any explicit mention of citizenship in his letters (see, however, the discussion of Paul's appeal to the Philippians regarding "citizenship in heaven" that is provided below in chapter 7) is thus not in tension with Luke's nuanced portrait of him as a "reluctant" Roman citizen in Acts.

4. See pp. 101–2 below for reflections upon the fact that Philippians and 2 Timothy, as well as the ending of Acts, image Paul as a chained prisoner in Rome.

5. Acts is silent regarding the identity of this emperor. Yet, inasmuch as Nero reigned from A.D. 54 to 68, it is virtually certain that he was the emperor in power when Paul arrived in Rome.

6

The Perspective of Paul in Romans and the Perspective of 1 Peter

ANALYSES OF CHRISTIANITY and the state have traditionally relied extensively on Paul's instructions in Romans 13:1–7. The present study will now consider these instructions but will situate them against the backdrop of Paul's journey from the status of free apostle to the status of chained Roman prisoner.[1] To this end, the present chapter begins with a section treating methodology and chronology and continues with a section examining Paul's personal context at the time he authored Romans. The next sections will analyze the essential elements in Paul's teaching in Romans 13:1–7 and the various factors that may possibly have influenced Paul to adopt this perspective. The final section will then consider Titus 3:1 and 1 Peter 2:13–14, passages in which the perspective resembles that of Romans 13.

CONSIDERATIONS REGARDING METHODOLOGY AND CHRONOLOGY

Up to this point, considerations relative to chronology have not loomed large in the present study. The perspective of John's Gospel has been placed alongside of the perspective of the Synoptic Gospels (particularly Luke), and the perspective of Acts has been positioned in proximity to these other two perspectives. No argument has been made that the perspective of John's Gospel is "later" or "earlier" than the perspective of Luke's Gospel or the Acts of the Apostles.

As regards the Pauline corpus, however, chronology is of decisive importance. A central thesis of the present study is that the undisputed letters of Paul disclose two widely varying perspectives regarding Roman rule, the "accommodative" perspective of Romans and the "resistant" perspective of Philippians. It is thus imperative to determine which letter Paul wrote first. Chapter 7 will argue that Philippians was written near the conclusion of Paul's ministry, considerably after the time of Romans. Philippians thus has the stronger claim to set forth Paul's ultimate perspective on the topic of Christians and Roman power.

The preceding paragraph does not address the methodological issues involved. What are the criteria for locating Romans chronologically well in advance of Philippians? How are Paul's other "undisputed" letters to be positioned in relation to Romans? What assessment is to be made of Colossians, Ephesians, and 2 Timothy, letters many scholars regard as having been written in Paul's name by his disciples? And what is the relationship between the portrait of Paul in his own letters from prison and the portrait of Paul as a Roman prisoner that Luke provides in Acts? The present chapter and chapter 7 will address these (and related) methodological questions in due course.

PAUL'S CONTEXT
AT THE TIME OF ROMANS

When he wrote to the Christians of Rome, Paul's *geographical* location was somewhere in the eastern provinces of the Roman empire, and several factors favor Corinth in Achaia. In terms of his *biographical* location, several references within the letter indicate that Paul is at a plateau in his journey as an apostle of Christ Jesus. In 15:19b he boldly asserts: "from Jerusalem and as far around as Illyricum, I have fully preached the Gospel of Christ." Then, in 15:23a, before indicating that he now intends to press forward to Spain by way of Jerusalem and Rome, he audaciously provides his rationale: "since I no longer have any room for work in these regions."

These statements seemingly serve to locate Paul's letter to the Romans after his letters to the communities of Thessalonica, Corinth, and Galatia. Paul considers his mission in these territories essentially completed; he no longer needs to be immediately engaged in nurturing the lives of these Christian communities. With confidence, he can leave them for a substantial time and press forward to the far horizons of Spain.

Note that nothing in these two statements (and nothing elsewhere in Romans) indicates that Paul has experienced *sustained* custody as a Roman prisoner. Nor is there anything in the text of Romans to suggest that Paul is anticipating that his future journeys will bring him into chained custody! Romans is not written by a prisoner in chains, and there is nothing in Romans to suggest that such an image of himself even exists remotely within Paul's consciousness.

There are additional points regarding Paul's context to be noted. First, as the text of the letter immediately makes clear, Paul is writing a magnificent systematic reflection on the deepest realities of Christian faith. Second he is writing to a Christian community that he himself has not founded. Third Paul hopes that the Roman Christians will respond generously to his needs as an apostle bound for Spain. Fourth, in the estimation of virtually all commentators on Romans, Nero was the reigning emperor at the time when Paul's letter reached Rome.

Paul's Instructions in Romans 13:1–7

In writing at such length to the Christians at Rome, Paul may have envisioned that his counsels and directives would circulate to other Christian communities beyond Rome. Indeed, the universal and unqualified way in which Paul frames his counsel lends support to the interpretation that, *at this stage of his discipleship,* Paul's was convinced that Christians in Rome and elsewhere in the empire should observe the directives and tax requirements of their Roman rulers without hesitation.

Paul's admonitions in Romans 13:1–7 can be structured in the following way. In v. 1a he states his fundamental counsel to be subject to the authorities. In vv. 1b–4, he presents the rationale for the position he has given in v. 1a, explaining in almost metaphysical terms that the authorities are instituted by God and function to further God's objectives. Verse 5 essentially repeats the admonition of v. 1 and refers to the two arguments that Paul has just made. In v. 6 Paul refers to Roman taxation and urges full compliance on the grounds that the authorities are God's ministers in this matter. Verse 7 again emphasizes the importance of being subject to the Roman authorities in taxation and in one's general mode of conduct.

In order to illustrate the care with which Paul has constructed his presentation and particularly to illuminate the way in which subjection to the Roman authorities is a thrice-repeated refrain of this passage, the full text of Paul's words is presented in the following manner:

Let every person be subject to the governing authorities. (v. 1a)

> For there is no authority except from God, and those that exist have been instituted by God. Therefore he who resists the authorities resists what God has appointed and those who resist will incur judgment. For rulers are not a terror to good conduct, but to bad. Would you have not fear of him who is in authority? Then do what is good and you will receive his approval, for he is God's appointed servant for your good. But if you do wrong, be afraid, for he does not bear the sword in vain; he is the servant of God to execute his wrath on the wrongdoer. (vv. 1b–4)

Therefore one must be subject not only to avoid God's wrath but also for the sake of conscience. (v. 5)

> For the same reason you also pay taxes, for the authorities are ministers of God attending to this very thing. Pay all of them their due, taxes to whom taxes are due, revenue to whom revenue is due. (vv. 6–7a)

(Pay) respect to whom respect is due, honor to whom honor is due (v. 7b).

Romans 13:1–7 has been extensively dissected and analyzed by Pauline scholars and may well be the most frequently commented

upon passage in the Pauline corpus. Some interpreters have pur-
ported to find nuances within Paul's vocabulary and phrasing that
would have the effect of severely limiting the thoroughgoing
accommodation that Paul's words, *prima facie,* appear to urge
here. Perhaps the most direct way to display the inadequacy of
such approaches is to project the response of the Roman authorities themselves to the broad concepts present within this passage.
As noted, Nero was almost certainly emperor when Paul's letter
arrived in Rome. Let Nero's putative reactions to the concepts and
counsels expressed in Romans 13:1–7 now be considered.

At least four features of Romans 13:1–7 would have elicited
Nero's enthusiasm, had this passage been brought to his attention.
Although Paul's phrasing is somewhat intricate, his fundamental
concepts emerge clearly and would be easily apparent to the
emperor just as they would be easily apparent to Paul's Christian
readers. These concepts regard: (a) the divine warrant for Roman
rule, (b) approval for the Roman authorities' use of the sword,
(c) the general requirement for Christians to be subject, and (d) a
particular emphasis on paying the imperial taxes.

First consider Nero's positive estimation of Paul's statement in
13:1b that there is no authority except from God and that "those
that exist have been instituted by God." (Since Paul's letter is sent
to the capital, Nero and the other high officials of the empire are
principally designated by Paul's various references to "the authorities.") Consider also Paul's reference in vv. 4 and 6b to the
(Roman) authorities as "servant(s) of God" and "ministers of God."
Given Nero's penchant for appropriating all available honorifics,
he would have found Paul's terminology here highly congenial. In
the same manner, note that Paul's words in vv. 4–6 regarding the
Roman authorities' benign use of the sword would have received
applause from any emperor.

Given these foundational concepts, Paul's logical conclusion
that a thoroughgoing subjection and a thoroughgoing deference
were incumbent upon Christians would not have been surprising
for Nero just as it would not have been surprising for Paul's Christian audience at Rome. This deference is specifically mandated in
the matter of taxation. Not only direct taxes but also the various
forms of indirect taxes are to be willingly paid. One only needs to

contrast Paul's instructions with those of Jesus according to Luke 20:25 to perceive the high degree of accommodation to Roman taxation that Paul here recommends. Christians who stood before Nero and echoed Jesus' response of Luke 20:25 could well expect to be charged with *maiestas*.[2] In contrast, Christians echoing Paul's directives in Romans 13:1–7 would only meet with imperial benevolence.

FACTORS POSSIBLY INFLUENCING PAUL'S PERSPECTIVE

What motivated Paul to recommend such an accommodative approach to the imperial authorities and their taxation? At least four factors can be identified as plausible influences on Paul, although in the end there is no certainty as to whether any of them had an impact. First, given the social and political turbulence involving the Jews of Rome, Paul may have been convinced that the Christians of Rome should distance themselves from all politically controversial conduct. Second, Paul may have been motivated by eschatological considerations. Third, the Jewish wisdom traditions that were available to Paul may have supplied him with the basic concepts of allegiance that he utilized for Romans 13. Finally, Paul's own personally high estimation for the achievements of the Roman empire may underpin the counsel he provides.

If Paul knew and attached importance to the fact that Jews had been expelled from Rome by an edict of Tiberius and again by an edict of Claudius, and if he was aware of protests in Rome against certain forms of imperial taxes, these historical factors may have influenced the framing of Romans 13:1–7. From Paul's other letters it is evident that the upbuilding of Christian community was always a high priority for him. Thus, in writing to the Christians in Rome, Paul may have judged that words encouraging them to cooperate with the imperial authorities with a view to building up their own community life were advisable. By consistently being subject and by paying all levied taxes, the Roman Christians would be safeguarded from expulsion and allowed to flourish in peace.

Although Romans does not have the eschatological urgency of 1 Thessalonians, Romans 13:11b–12a, a passage that is proximate to 13:1–7, indicates that Paul still envisioned Christ's return in the not distant future. Given this eschatological perspective, it would have been plausible for Paul to advise the Roman Christians to follow the course of least resistance in dealing with the imperial authorities. Since Christ was soon to return, it was inadvisable for them to put time, energy, and livelihood into controversies with the Roman authorities regarding taxation and other imperial demands.

Because he was well versed in his Jewish heritage, Paul presumably knew the various Jewish wisdom sayings that (a) linked the authority of the existing political rulers to the authority of God and (b) connected the rulers' use of the sword with the accomplishment of God's punishment (see Prov. 24:21–22, for example). Clearly, such concepts from the Jewish wisdom tradition could have influenced Paul's ideas and his language in Romans 13:1–7. Nevertheless, if Paul did choose to draw upon this aspect of his Jewish heritage, he was not *compelled* to do so. For conceivably he may have chosen to reflect other, more revolutionary currents from within Jewish tradition. For example, he might have availed himself of concepts from the earlier Maccabean rebellion or from the contemporaneous insurgency against Roman rule fomented by the Zealots.

At this stage of his journey, what was Paul's personal valuation of the Roman empire? Significantly, the first two factors that have just been considered, Paul's concern for the upbuilding of the Christian community and his sensitivity to eschatology would not necessarily presuppose a positive assessment of Rome and its rulers by Paul. In other words, Paul could have set forth Romans 13:1–7 as prudent counsel even though he did not personally esteem the Roman authorities or their empire.

On the other hand, in authoring these verses, Paul's own personal judgment may have been that the Roman authorities were actually playing a positive role in bringing about peace and order within the territories of the empire. In support of such an interpretation, consider Paul's declaration in Romans 15:19 that he has already preached the Gospel faithfully "from Jerusalem and as far around as Illyricum." Conceivably, Paul valued the Roman provincial system as a necessary condition for his successful ministry. He had traveled over well-maintained Roman roads and profited from the Roman communications network; he had benefited from navigable ports and waterways; the ordering presence of the Roman military had protected him on land from brigands and on sea from piracy.

Significantly, when he authored Romans 13:1–7, Paul had not experienced the privation of *extended* Roman custody. In his later letters, the aspect of sustained custody in Roman chains will loom large for Paul; but, prior to Romans, the hardships he experienced, serious and indeed life-threatening as they were, were hardships that occurred in great measure apart from the Roman system. Even when Paul lists the sufferings he has endured (2 Cor. 11:23 catalogues "far more imprisonments, with countless beatings"), the sense is that these prison experiences were ad hoc and limited in duration. Even if Roman officers or Rome-approved local authorities perpetrated these maltreatments, these *temporary* penalties and imprisonments are to be distinguished from the officially authorized, extended custody, replete with chains, that Paul would subsequently experience.

In effect, prior to Romans, Paul had not yet experienced the Roman system operating against him (!) in a significant way. It is possible that his own experiences as a traveler within the eastern provinces had been sufficiently positive to elicit Paul's respect and even his admiration for the Roman system and the authorities who controlled it. According to this view, Paul's instructions to the Roman Christians to support the Roman authorities thus arose from his own conviction that the Roman system deserved to be supported.

In summary, four factors (concern regarding turbulence involving the Jews of Rome, eschatological considerations, an appreciation for Jewish loyalty traditions, and positive personal experiences with the Roman system) have now been identified as possible influences impelling Paul to the perspective that he set forth in Romans 13. Nevertheless, in the end, none of these factors, solely or in combination, can be taken as a certain influ-

ence on Paul's perspective. For Paul may have adopted the stance
of accommodation in Roman 13:1-7 for reasons that still have not
been identified. Romans 13:1–7 does counsel a remarkable thoroughgoing compliance to those who received it: that much is
certain. *Why* Paul adopted this approach is still far from being
determined.

NOTEWORTHY PASSAGES FROM 1 PETER, TITUS, AND 1 TIMOTHY

Within the canon of the New Testament, three other letters contain passages that, to varying degrees, present perspectives that
resemble the perspective of Romans 13:1–7. Two of these passages
occur in Titus and 1 Timothy, letters whose attribution to Paul is
disputed. The third passage occurs in 1 Peter, a letter whose
authorship is also disputed.

Here the specific methodology being followed in the present
study again functions decisively. For, in effect, the uncertainties
concerning the authorship and the dates of these three letters will
be set aside. Instead each letter will be considered simply as a first-
century document that offers counsel to Christians regarding their
responses to Roman power.[3]

Because they can be treated more briefly, it is well to begin with
the relevant passages from Titus and 1 Timothy. Both of these passages have a conceptual resemblance to Romans 13 in the sense
that both advocate a cooperative stance regarding the Roman
authorities.[4] It should specifically be noted that the same Greek
verb (*hypotassō*) that is used in Romans 13:1, 5 is employed also in
Titus 3:1. (It appears also in the citations from 1 Peter that will be
made below.) This verb is variously translated in the RSV as "be
subject" or "be submissive": "Remind them to be submissive to
rulers and authorities, to be obedient, to be ready for any honest
work" (Titus 3:1).

The passage from 1 Timothy provides a counsel regarding the
Roman authorities that is not present in Romans 13. 1 Timothy
asks its readers to pray on behalf of these Roman authorities. Significantly, 1 Timothy supplies a rationale for such prayers and

intercessions: they are offered so that Christians will be able to lead quiet and peaceful lives under these authorities. As noted above, this rationale is not expressly stated in Romans 13 but may have been Paul's unstated rationale. The following is the counsel of 1 Timothy:

> First of all, then, I urge that supplications, prayers, intercessions, and thanksgivings be made for all, for kings and all who are in high positions, that we may lead a quiet and peaceable life, godly and respectful in every way. (2:1–2, author's translation)

Before noting an important consideration that pertains to the status of Titus and 1 Timothy in this study, one additional consideration that is particular to 1 Timothy is appropriately made here. Written, as it assuredly was, in a social context in which a quasi-divine status was being claimed by, and/or claimed on behalf of, various emperors, 1 Timothy's majestic acclamations on behalf of God's surpassing sovereignty are remarkable. Shortly after its opening, 1 Timothy acclaims "the only God" as unending "king of ages" (1:17). Later, at the close of the letter, the following wording appears (6:15): "and this (the 'epiphany' of the Lord Jesus Christ) will be made manifest at the proper time by the blessed and only sovereign, the King of kings and Lord of lords."

A methodological point pertaining to the present study's perspective on Titus and 1 Timothy needs mention. Whether they were written in Paul's name by a disciple, or whether they were authored by Paul himself, the image of Paul projected in both of these letters is that of "Paul unfettered by chains." As a consequence, the counsel that these letters set forth relative to the Roman authorities should not be regarded as the counsel of a chained Roman prisoner.

The present study thus distinguishes sharply between Titus and 1 Timothy, on the one hand, and 2 Timothy on the other just as it distinguishes sharply between Romans on the one hand and Philemon and Philippians on the other. Chapter 7 will develop the implications of this disjunction between letters that image Paul in chains and letters that do not. It can be stated here that the counsel of Paul regarding the Roman authorities in Titus is superseded by the counsel given by Paul as a chained prisoner in Philippians.

A third canonical passage whose counsel resembles that of Romans 13:1–7 is 1 Peter 2:13–17, a passage appearing in a letter written to Christians living in five Roman provinces in Asia Minor. This letter announces in its first verse that it is authored by Peter, Christ's apostle, and indicates that it is being sent "to the exiles of the Dispersion in Pontus, Galatia, Cappadocia, Asia, and Bithynia."[5] In 5:13 the author closes with greetings from "she who is at Babylon, who is likewise chosen." This reference may specifically identify Rome as the letter's place of origin, or it may indicate more generally that the author's community lives in "exile" just as the recipients of the letter live in "exile."[6] The actual relationship between the author and his readers is not specified. The letter indicates the author's general familiarity with the stressful circumstances of his addressees. Whether his knowledge of their circumstances is derived from his own ministry with them or from the reports of others remains uncertain.

The analysis of 2:13–17 will establish that the author views the Roman system favorably and encourages cooperation with the Roman authorities. However, before proceeding to a consideration of this important passage, the question of whether the author of Peter envisions the recipients of his letter to be experiencing social harassment and/or some form of persecution involving the Roman authorities needs to be addressed.

Conceivably, the "various trials" (1:6) and the "fiery ordeal" (4:12) mentioned in the letter refer exclusively to discrimination and other types of socio-economic harassment.[7] Other passages in the letter do, in fact, establish that Christians are being reviled by members of the surrounding populace (2:12, 15; 3:9, 16; 4:4). Nevertheless, the letter's repeated references to Jesus' trial, his rejection, and his death (2:23–24a; 3:18; 4:1) raise the possibility that the situation is more severe.

Does 1 Peter actually envision that formal Roman trials are in the offing? In 3:15–16 the author advises his readers about the need to have a defense (*apologia*) prepared and counsels that, in their hearts, they are to hold fast to a reverence for Christ "*as Lord.*"[8] Further, in presenting their defense they are to conduct themselves "with gentleness and reverence" as a means of refuting the unprincipled denunciations of their opponents. Such counsel might well prove useful at trials before the imperial authorities, but its presence in the letter does not ipso facto establish a situation of official imperial trials. Conceivably the situation that the author is addressing is one of harassment from the surrounding populace with the *possibility* of delations that would bring about the official involvement of the provincial authorities.

In addition to providing the disciples in Asia Minor with instructions for their discipleship at critical moments, 1 Peter also sets forth counsel for their ongoing dealings with the Roman authorities. 1 Peter 2:13–17, the passage referred to at the outset of this section, provides this counsel:

> Be subject for the Lord's sake to every human institution, whether it be to the emperor as supreme, or to governors as sent by him to punish those who do wrong and praise those who do right. For it is God's will that by doing right you should put to silence the ignorance of the foolish. Live as free persons, yet without using your freedom as a pretext for evil; but live as servants of God. Honor everyone. Love the brethren. Fear God. Honor the emperor. (author's translation)

The counsel expressed in these verses resembles the counsel expressed in Romans 13:1–7 while differing from it in degree. Significantly, 1 Peter is favorably disposed toward the workings of the Roman provincial system which functions "to punish those who do wrong and praise those who do right."[9] As a consequence the author urges his readers to *be subject* to the Roman emperor as supreme and to the governors sent by him.[10]

In 2:13–17, v. 15 supplies the motivation for the respectful subservience that the author recommends. However, to appreciate the author's meaning in 2:15 properly, it is necessary to note that in 2:12 he has already expressed a comparable perspective. As is immediately clear, both of these verses suppose that good conduct will have a positive influence upon the situation:

> Maintain good conduct among the Gentiles, so that in case they speak against you as wrongdoers, they may see your good deeds and glorify God on the day of visitation. (1 Pet. 2:12)

> For it is God's will that by doing right you should put to silence the ignorance of foolish men. (1 Pet. 2:15)

The principal task remaining is to integrate the meaning of 2:15 with the larger meaning of 2:13–17. This task can be readily accomplished by establishing that the conduct envisioned by the phrase "doing right" in 2:15 actually is specified in vv. 13–14 and vv. 16–17.

If they comply with their provincial governors, and if they take care to *honor*[11] the emperor, then these Christians will establish (for the authorities) that the charges brought by their opponents are baseless.[12] By following such a course, the Christians of Asia Minor will thus be able to continue in their life of faith, a life in which they honor everyone, love the brotherhood and fear God (2:17).

For the sake of completeness, one additional element in the counsel of 1 Peter needs to be considered. When the Christians of these provinces, despite their best efforts, find themselves unjustly treated, they are called to manifest a steadfast faithfulness in the face of this suffering. They are to take Jesus himself as their exemplar for such a response. For he himself faced unjust condemnation and death without manifesting hatred or vindictiveness (3:17–18). This same pattern of nonvengeful endurance of unjust suffering is strongly emphasized in another part of the letter in which Christian slaves are counseled, in vocabulary that is similar to that used in the book of Revelation, to "endure patiently" (1 Pet. 2:20b) the unjust beatings inflicted by their masters. In striving to do this, they are to take heart from the example of Jesus: "When he was reviled, he did not revile in return; when he suffered, he did not threaten; but he trusted to him who judges justly" (1 Pet. 2:23).

In summary, 1 Peter provides Christian slaves who face unjust treatment from their masters and Christians who are subject to unjust treatment from the surrounding populace and/or the Roman authorities with essentially the same counsel. In both cases, those unjustly afflicted are to find encouragement and strength in the example of Jesus. For Jesus, trusting himself to God's vindication, patiently endured his sufferings without reviling those who inflicted them.

Finally, it should be noted that no critical word is expressed regarding those "responsible" for the evil in either of these situations. 1 Peter does not express a critical word regarding (or to) the owners of these Christian slaves. Similarly, the letter expresses no critical word against the Roman governors of these provinces for failing to curb the negative behavior of those inflicting harm upon the Christians. Some interpreters of the letter hold that the author's closing reference to Babylon (5:13) expresses a criticism of the imperial order.[13] However, as noted above, "Babylon" does not necessarily designate the empire or its capital. Further, the letter's comments regarding the Roman system in 2:13–17 are so explicitly favorable that it is difficult to conceive that the author now desires to image Rome as the epitome of decadence and oppression.

NOTES

1. The first five sections of the present chapter summarize the analysis made in chapter 5 of my forthcoming study, *Paul in Chains: The Impact of Roman Imprisonment in the Letters of Paul* (New York: Crossroad, 2001).

2. It was noted in chapter 3 that Jesus' "evaluative" reply to the question regarding tribute would not have been satisfactory to the Roman authorities.

3. If it is judged that Paul and Peter did not author these letters, the counsel of their anonymous authors regarding the Roman authorities is still to be taken seriously as "canonical" counsel. It will be suggested in chapter 9 below that second-century Christians be imaged reading and considering the counsel of all of the canonical texts.

4. The phrase "conceptual resemblance" is used advisedly here. In the estimation of many scholars, the attitude the Roman authorities expressed in 1 Timothy and Titus is "derived" from the counsel of Romans 13:1–7. In contrast, the present study presumes no direct link between Romans 13 and these two letters.

5. J. Elliott sagely notes that questions regarding the authorship and location of 1 Peter are intertwined with a range of other questions concerning, for example, the traditions the letter incorporates, its relationship to other New Testament writings, and the position of the Roman empire toward Christianity at its time of composition (*A Home for the Homeless* [Philadelphia: Fortress, 1981], 270–71). For an extended discussion of these and other related issues, see P. Achtemeier, *1 Peter* (Minneapolis: Fortress, 1996), 1–75.

From the standpoint of the present study, it is significant that Christians in the province of Asia are among those addressed by 1 Peter. It will be observed in chapter 8 below that the book of Revelation addresses seven Christian churches within this same province. Are Christians of the same generation addressed in both cases? If so, they receive widely divergent counsel from 1 Peter and Revelation regarding the Roman authorities. This divergence will be explicated and emphasized in chapter 9 below.

6. L. Goppelt (*A Commentary on I Peter* [Grand Rapids: Eerdmans, 1993], 47–48, 373–77) and P. Achtemeier (*1 Peter*, 353–55) both regard 5:13 as referencing the Christian community located in Rome. J. N. Kelly leans toward this interpretation, but, influenced by M.-É. Boismard and K. Heussi, also recognizes the possibility that "Babylon" may designate any place where a Christian community is experiencing "exile" (*A Commentary on the Epistles of Peter and Jude* [New York: Harper & Row, 1969], 217–20).

If 1 Peter were written not from Rome but from some other location (of "exile"), then from where? In "Pierre (Première Epître de)," in *Dictionnaire de la Bible*, Supplement VII (Paris: Letouzey & Ané, 1966), col. 1453, M.-É. Boismard suggests Antioch in Syria as the place where this letter reached its final form.

7. After a discussion of the persecution of the Christians by Nero, Domitian, and Trajan, P. Achtemeier contends that the persecutions faced by readers of 1 Peter were principally due to unofficial harassment by the local populace (*1 Peter*, 35–36). C. Talbert similarly contends that these sufferings are from unofficial oppression as opposed to state persecution and discusses the ways in which the Christian lifestyle could have generated fear and repression from the larger society ("The Place of I Peter," in *Perspectives on First Peter* [Macon, Ga.: Mercer University Press, 1986], 145).

8. Achtemeier notes the forensic connotations of *apologia* and several of the other terms used here and provides a short excursus on 1 Peter 3:15–16 with reference to the Pliny–Trajan correspondence (*1 Peter*, 232–35). As Achtemeier points out, these same concepts would also be relevant for Christians if they were faced with informal accusations and demands.

9. Goppelt (*A Commentary on I Peter*, 190) and especially Achtemeier (*1 Peter*, 180–82) rightly observe that Romans 13:1–7 is more thoroughgoing in its support of the Roman authorities than 1 Peter 2:13–17 is. Nevertheless, *in its own right*, 1 Peter 2:13–17 positively appreciates the Roman system and accords substantive support for the emperor and the Roman provincial authorities.

10. Given the analysis made in chapter 3 above, the assertions made by such commentators as Goppelt (*A Commentary on I Peter*, 180–81) and Achtemeier (*1 Peter*, 180) that 1 Peter 2:13–17 reflects Jesus' teaching regarding compliance with Roman rule must be rigorously criticized. Goppelt (p. 181), following G. Delling, even goes so far as to aver that Romans 13:1–7 accurately interprets the Synoptic tribute passages!

11. J. N. Kelly discusses the counsel of honoring (*timate*) the emperor noting that it is juxtaposed with the counsel to honor "everyone" (*Epistles of Peter and Jude*, 112–13). Goppelt comments that inasmuch as this passage accords honor but not "fear" to the emperor it lends less support to the Roman authorities than Romans 13:7 does (*A Commentary on 1 Peter*, 190). For the wording of Romans 13:7 is such as to suggest that "fear" as well as "honor" may appropriately be given to these authorities.

12. The logic expressed in 1 Peter 2:15 should be juxtaposed with the logic expressed by the author of 1 Timothy at 2:1–2 (as discussed above). 1 Timothy envisions that the Roman authorities will be positively affected by the *supplications* and *prayers* offered by Christians. 1 Peter envisions that the *right conduct* of Christians will influence the Roman authorities to disregard any complaints against these Christians. Thus, in both cases, in contrast with Romans 13:1–7, a strategy for dealing with the authorities is expressly articulated.

13. In the view of Goppelt, this closing reference to Babylon is a symbolic reference to Rome as the locus of imperial power and persecution (*A Commentary on I Peter*, 20; see also 373–75). Goppelt holds that the author of the letter consciously emphasizes this negative image of imperial Rome even though he appreciates the Roman system and urges cooperation with it at 2:13–17.

7

The Perspective of Paul in Chains

T HE ANALYSIS OF THE PRESENT CHAPTER is extremely important for the broad argument of this book.[1] Essentially the
thesis propounded in this chapter is that the perspective of
Paul as a Roman prisoner in chains is not the perspective of Paul
the author of the letter to the Romans. In Romans 13:1–7, Paul's
approach was to counsel accommodation to the Roman authorities. In Philippians, as will be seen, Paul is concerned to highlight
the standard of heavenly citizenship and to insist that the Roman
authorities are themselves subject to the sovereign rule of Jesus.

Considerations regarding chronology are clearly significant for
this chapter's thesis. For this reason, the first section takes up the
question of the sequence of Paul's last undisputed letters. Section
two then undertakes a brief analysis of Paul's references to his
chains in his letter to Philemon. At considerably greater length,
the next sections examine Paul's developed perspective in Philippians, Colossians, Ephesians, and 2 Timothy, three letters of disputed authorship that, in different ways, image Paul in chains. The
final section of this chapter is a brief examination of Paul's
surroundings in Philippians in comparison with his location in
2 Timothy and his location at the end of the Acts of the Apostles.

CHRONOLOGY AND LOCATION

The letter to Philemon and the letter to the Philippians are filled with references to Paul's chains and to other aspects of his custody and for this reason have long been designated as "prison letters." There is virtually universal agreement among biblical scholars that Paul himself authored these letters, but there is little agreement about the time and place of authorship.

In the view of this study, the *extended* imprisonment that is attested to in each letter is a decisive factor for positioning both of these letter after Romans. In writing to Philemon, Paul provides various indications of the fact that he has been in chains for some while. He has had time to "beget" Onesimus as his spiritual child (v. 10). His closing greeting also implies that there has been sufficient time for a support circle to develop around him (vv. 23–24). Perhaps most memorably, Paul has been in chains for such an extended period of time that his image of himself has become that of "a prisoner for Christ Jesus" (vv. 1, 9).

In a variety of ways, Philippians also testifies to a situation of extended custody. Paul is "accustomed" to his confinement and is prepared to continue as a prisoner until the time when a decisive verdict will be given in his case. He is able to speak easily and articulately about his situation (1:7b; 2:23). He has been kept in chains long enough for the explanation of his situation to circulate "throughout the whole praetorian guard and to all the rest" (1:13a). Paul has been in custody long enough for the Philippians to learn of it and send Epaphroditus to assist him only to have Epaphroditus fall sick (2:25–30). A sufficient amount of time has elapsed to enable tensions to emerge within the Christian community in terms of divergent responses to Paul the prisoner (1:14–18). Clearly, these developments can be thought of as overlapping one another. Nevertheless, even if they all occurred within the same year or years, an extended interval in ongoing custody is still presumed.

The fact that Paul seriously contemplates a possible death verdict in Philippians (1:20; 2:17; 2:23) suggests that Philippians was

written at a later date than Philemon. In Philemon Paul is somewhat optimistic regarding his presumed release (v. 22), and there is
no mention that he has earlier been close to a capital verdict.
Would Paul have expressed himself in this way if he had earlier
been so proximate to death? Conversely, the repeated references to
the prospect of his death in Philippians make good sense if it is
assumed that Paul's earlier situation (the situation reflected in
Philemon) has taken a turn for the worse. Additionally, the fact
that Paul is so isolated in Philippians (2:19–22) fits well with the
supposition that circumstances have separated him from the supporters who were with him at the time of Philemon. It is more
difficult to envision that, having lamented his isolation in Philippians, Paul then experienced a surfeit of support: the arrival of
Onesimus and five other reliable associates (Phlm. 23–24).

For various reasons, Rome must be regarded as the location for
Philippians. Paul's reference to "the whole praetorian guard and to
all the rest" (1:13a) has already been mentioned. In 4:22 he closes
the letter with the communication of greetings from the Christians among "Caesar's household." In terms of judicial procedure,
cases involving extended imprisonment and a capital verdict
would normally receive their definitive resolution in Rome.
Fourth, a Roman venue makes possible a plausible interpretation
for the notoriously difficult statements in 1:14–18. Admittedly,
this last factor involves a degree of circularity. Nevertheless, a
venue in Rome enables these verses to be interpreted in a far more
persuasive fashion than is the case with a venue in Caesarea or a
venue in Ephesus. Indeed, when all four of the factors just identified are cumulatively considered, it emerges that claims for Ephesus (in particular) and Caesarea can scarcely be sustained.

Once Philemon and Philippians, with their images of extended
imprisonment, are juxtaposed with Romans, with its image of an
energetic apostle bound for Spain, via Jerusalem and Rome, it
emerges that a Romans–Philemon–Philippians sequence best
accommodates the internal contents of these three letters. If Paul
had experienced sustained custody and had come to identify himself as a prisoner in chains, it is unlikely that these aspects would
have passed completely without mention in Romans. Second, it is
nearly inconceivable that Paul could have written Romans 13:1–7

if he had already experienced sustained imprisonment and come near to a sentence of death. (Recall that within the empire, only the Roman authorities have the power to effect sustained imprisonment and/or a sentence of death.) There is also the matter of the collection mentioned so prominently in Romans 15:25–28. Is it imaginable that his sustained imprisonment had occurred prior to all of his efforts on behalf of this collection?

In comparison, a Romans–Philemon–Philippians sequence accounts for these factors in a much more satisfactory fashion. Paul never refers to his imprisonment in the sixteen chapters of Romans because it had not yet occurred. His endeavors on behalf of the Jerusalem collection were undertaken and completed during the period of his free apostleship. And he gave the counsel of Romans 13:1–7 prior to his experience of sustained custody at the hand of the Roman authorities. Finally, a remarkable (paradoxical) implication of a Roman venue for Philippians is that Paul actually arrived in the capital of the empire not as a free apostle bound for Spain but rather as a prisoner in chains. In doing so, he proved to be a controversial figure for some of the Christians in Rome, persons who were presumably among the audience for his earlier magisterial letter.

PAUL, A PRISONER OF THE ROMAN AUTHORITIES, WRITES TO PHILEMON

The heading for this section is, by design, phrased to underscore the surprising circumstances in which the Letter to Philemon was authored. Prior to the arrival of Paul's letter, did Philemon and those associated with him know that Paul had been placed in chains? Did Philemon have any idea that Onesimus, the slave who had formerly served him (Philemon) was now at Paul's side and had become a Christian under Paul's sponsorship? Although neither of these questions can be answered from the available data, posing both of them helps to shed light on the rhetorical strategy Paul used in writing to his close friend Philemon.

Paul's reference to himself as a prisoner (vv. 1, 9) bound with chains (vv. 10, 13) combined with references to Timothy, Onesimus, and five others (vv. 23, 24) as supporters who are able to assist

him suggest that Paul was under a form of "military custody."
Although they are not mentioned explicitly in the letter, Philemon
would have presumed the presence of Roman soldiers as the super-
visors of Paul's custody. Further, these soldiers assuredly guarded
Paul under the authority of higher Roman officials. It should also
be noted that nowhere in the letter does Paul protest the treatment
that he is receiving. He does not challenge what has occurred, nor
does he denounce the conditions of his custody. His hope is to be
soon released from his confinement (v. 22), but nowhere does he
indicate, even subtlely, that he has been victimized by improper
procedures.

What then is Paul's rhetorical strategy in writing a letter that
may have had to pass the censorship of those guarding him? Paul
takes the route of utter directness with respect to the fact that
Philemon and others might be disoriented by, or even scandalized
by, Paul's circumstances. In his very first words, Paul boldly
announces that he is a prisoner and immediately sets forth the
explanation for this startling development: he is a prisoner "for
Christ Jesus." Paul has no need to state explicitly that he is a
Roman prisoner. Sustained imprisonment in the world of Philemon and Paul could only be an imprisonment that was mandated
by the Roman authorities. There are thus two principal rhetorical
achievements in Paul's opening words. Paul discloses the fact that
he is indeed a (Roman) prisoner. However, this condition is not due
to any fall from grace on his part. Rather, in an astonishing way,
Paul's chains are for the sake of Jesus his sovereign Lord.

When the text of the entire letter is carefully analyzed, it
emerges that Paul's principal objective in writing to Philemon is to
secure the manumission of Onesimus. In effect, Paul is arguing
that Onesimus should not literally or figuratively be returned to
the chains that Paul himself now wears. Paul advances this appeal
on more than one front. He makes reference to the fact that Philemon is indebted to Paul for his own life in Christ. He offers to
repay personally anything that Onesimus may owe Philemon. And
very significantly Paul focuses attention on the suffering that he
presently endures. This is done most memorably in v. 9 when Paul
poignantly points out that he is making his appeal as "an old man
and now a prisoner for Christ Jesus." The words "and now" testify

to Paul's own pondering of divine providence as it relates to the unanticipated event that has befallen him, the event of his imprisonment.

Paul also remarks that Onesimus has become a dear child to him precisely "in my chains" (v. 10). His closing reference to Epaphras as "my fellow prisoner" (v. 23) contributes significantly to the *Paulusbild* of the letter. For, by closing in this manner, Paul again brings to the fore that he is now Paul, the chained prisoner. As they read his letter from start to finish, this was the image of Paul that Philemon and his household would inescapably encounter; this image is present in every part of the letter.

As mentioned previously, there is nothing within this brief letter to suggest that Paul considered himself to be facing a death verdict. On the contrary, he envisions his release in the relatively near future although he cannot be certain of the timing of his release or even that it will occur (v. 22). In effect, the letter conveys that Paul will remain in his chains—without Onesimus' valued assistance—for as long as it is required of him. He does hope for release from this bondage, but in the meantime he will continue faithfully in the witness that has been entrusted to him.

THE PERSPECTIVE OF PHILIPPIANS

Philippians, like Philemon, may have been subject to censorship. If Philippians was subject to imperial review, it is remarkable that Paul was able to address the topic of Christian allegiance to the Roman order in as challenging a fashion as he does. Paul's custody is being supervised by members of the praetorian guard. He faces a decisive verdict of death or life, a decision that would be rendered by a high imperial court, probably by Nero himself. Nevertheless, he sets forth trenchant, albeit indirect, criticisms of the Roman social order. He boldly announces that the Roman authorities themselves are obligated to bend their knees before Jesus. And he counsels the Philippian Christians (who are also Roman citizens) that their highest allegiance is allegiance to Jesus and that their highest standard is the standard of citizenship in heaven.

It should not be thought that Philippians is only about the questions of Christian attitudes toward the emperor and the Roman social order. For example, Paul is obviously concerned to reconcile a conflict between two prominent women members of the Philippian community (4:2–3), and he warns against opponents who apparently are striving to impose the Jewish law upon the Gentile Christians at Philippi (3:2–3). Paul also wishes to thank the Philippians for their generosity in sending Epaphras to assist him (3:25–30), and throughout the letter he takes care to assuage any worry that his Philippian friends might have regarding Paul's own suffering.

Nevertheless, four major passages in the letter demonstrate that the question of Jesus' sovereignty and Christian comportment with the Roman order are very much on Paul's mind. His concepts and his nuanced phrasing in each of these major passages establish that his outlook has changed dramatically in comparison with his outlook at the time of Romans 13:1–7. In writing Philippians Paul, of course, does not systematically set aside the directives of Romans 13:1–7. Rather, he persuasively articulates a new set of concepts that have the effect of qualifying and superseding the premises and the counsel of Romans 13.

It is possible to present the analysis of this section by proceeding chronologically through Philippians. However, in order to grasp quickly the distinctiveness of Philippians, it is useful to begin immediately with the christological hymn that appears in chapter 2 of the letter. Whether or not Paul authored 2:6–11 himself or elected to include verses from a preexisting hymn, what must be recognized is that these verses decisively proclaim to the Philippians the unsurpassed sovereignty of Jesus *after* they have stressed his humiliating death by decree of the Roman authorities.

In 2:6–7 Paul reminds his Philippian audience of Jesus' downward-status path as he left equality with God to take the human form and the form of a servant. Consider now vv. 8–11. Jesus' downward status to death "even death on a cross" is emphasized. But then the upward movement to complete sovereignty is wonderfully announced:

> And being found in human form he humbled himself and became
> obedient unto death, even death on a cross. Therefore God has

highly exalted him and bestowed on him the name which is above every name, that at the name of Jesus every knee should bow, in heaven and on earth and under the earth, and every tongue confess that Jesus Christ is Lord, to the glory of God the Father. (2:8–11)

Jesus' humiliating death was decreed by the Roman authorities. What is now to be the response of the Roman authorities to Jesus as sovereign Lord? What is to be the response of Nero, the reigning Roman ruler to the sovereignty of Jesus as Lord? These direct questions elucidate a key aspect of the meaning that Paul is now communicating to his friends at Philippi, friends who are Roman citizens and well familiar with the patterns of the empire and the claims of the emperor. Shall not Nero bend his knee at the name of Jesus? Shall not Nero confess the surpassing Lordship of Jesus? Paul's repeated use of the modifier "every" allows for no exceptions. *Every* being, including Nero and every other Roman authority, is ultimately subject to Jesus.

The second major passage to be considered, 3:17–4:1, also contains a significant reference to the unequaled sovereignty of Jesus. Near the end of this passage Paul asserts that Jesus holds the power "which enables him to subject all things to himself." In Romans 13:1 and 13:5, Paul used *hypotassō*, the verb for "being subject," in reference to the need for Christians to subject themselves fully to the Roman authorities. Here obviously his thrust is far different. Paul's emphasis now is that Jesus alone is truly sovereign; he alone has the power to subject all things to him.

The meaning of 3:18–19 has long been controverted, but there are substantial grounds for interpreting these verses as expressing Paul's disdain for the sexual licentiousness of Nero and his confederates, especially in Rome. Earlier in the letter, in 2:15–16, Paul gave a critique of the moral bankruptcy of the Roman milieu in which he and the Philippians are situated, calling upon his audience to be "blameless and innocent, children of God without blemish in the midst of a crooked and perverse generation, among whom you shine as lights in the world."

Philippians 3:18–19 can thus be regarded as an elaboration and a specification of this earlier critique. Writing as a supervised prisoner, Paul does not identify Nero or any other high Roman ruler by name or office; nevertheless these authorities are the object of his critique. Because they utterly disdain responsible conduct and have the power to seduce and coerce others into their mode of behavior, these officials are truly "enemies of the cross of Christ." Their great power makes them virtually unaccountable for the heinous deeds they perpetrate. The entire situation is such that Paul is grieved and frustrated to the point of tears. Here then are his words decrying this state of affairs:

> For many, of whom I have often told you and now tell you even with tears, live as enemies of the cross of Christ. Their end is destruction, their god is the sexual organ, and they glory in their shame, with minds set on earthly things. (3:18–19, author's translation)

Having trenchantly decried the social milieu prevailing in the highly "Roman" settings of Philippi and Rome (again the significance of Philippi as a colony of Roman citizens), Paul then encourages the Roman citizens of Philippi to look beyond the standards of Roman citizenship to the true standards of "citizenship" (*politeuma*) in heaven. It is from heaven, after all, that Jesus, the true *Savior*, exercises his sovereignty. And in specific contrast to the Roman authorities, who excel in the degradation of the human body, Jesus alone has sovereign power to transform the fragile human body into an incorruptible body of glory. Paul's actual phrasing is as follows: "But our citizenship is in heaven, and from it we await a Savior, the Lord Jesus Christ, who will change our lowly body to be like his glorious body, by the power which enables him even to subject all things to himself" (3:20–21, author's translation).

In 4:1 Paul concludes with a warm exhortation to his beloved Philippians to "stand firm thus in the Lord." A similar exhortation, "stand firm in one spirit," occurs earlier in the letter, in 1:27c. Significantly, 1:27 also includes *politeuesthe,* a verb form derived from the same root as the noun for citizenship that appears in 3:20. (These two politically oriented words both occur only in Philippians among Paul's undisputed letters; yet such vocabulary is not unexpected, given that Paul is writing from the political capital of the empire to Christians who are located in a provincial city with extremely close ties to Rome.) Paul's idea in 1:27 is once again that the Philippians must take the standards of their heavenly Lord as a guide for conduct in their social and civic lives. In this passage Paul presumes that his Philippian readers are experiencing something of the struggle that he himself is facing. He encourages his hearers not to be frightened or intimidated, because their opponents are headed to *destruction* while the Christian future is *salvation.*

> Only let your civic living be worthy of the gospel of Christ, so that whether I come and see you or am absent, I may hear of you that you stand firm in one spirit, with one mind striving side by side for the faith of the gospel, and not frightened in anything by your opponents. This is a clear omen to them of their destruction, but of your salvation, and that from God. For it has been granted to you that for the sake of Christ you should not only believe in him but also suffer for his sake, engaged in the same conflict which you saw and now hear to be mine. (Phil. 1:27–30, author's translation)

Philippians 3:7–11, the fourth major passage to be considered, has been kept for last because it may contain a partial explanation for the new perspective regarding the Roman authorities that Paul is manifesting in Philippians. The passage as a whole is permeated with Paul's testimony of his intense commitment to Jesus.

Paul is in the capital city of "lord Nero," but it is to Jesus that Paul proclaims his devotion and allegiance. Paul says nothing to indicate that he opposes Nero's rule, but it is to Jesus that his primary allegiance is given. Earlier Paul has described Jesus as having had equality with God and has testified that Jesus has been given a name that is above every name. Now Paul simply avows his personal closeness to Jesus. He refers to him as "*my* Lord" (the only instance of such usage within his letters) and emphasizes that Jesus is everything to him: "But whatever gain I had, I counted as loss for the sake of Christ. Indeed I count everything as loss because of the surpassing worth of knowing Christ Jesus my Lord" (3:7–8a).

In rhapsodic language Paul continues this reflection regarding his bondedness with Jesus. He expressed his commitment to suffer the loss of all things, trusting in the power of Christ's resurrection. From the perspective of this study, Paul's expressed willingness to share Christ's suffering, even to the point of *"becoming like him in his death,"* is extremely significant. Before presenting an analysis of the meaning of this phrase, it is useful to consider it in its context:

> For his sake I have suffered the loss of all things, and count them as refuse, in order that I may gain Christ and be found in him, not having a righteousness of my own, based on law, but that which is through faith in Christ, the righteousness from God that depends on faith; that I may know him and the power of his resurrection, and may share his sufferings, becoming like him in his death, that if possible I may attain the resurrection from the dead. (3:8b–11)

Paul's ultimate desire is to be with Christ in the life of the resurrection. Death in some form is the necessary prelude to this fuller union with Paul's Lord—Paul has long known that. However, the insight that Paul now broaches is that he may actually be called to suffer death in the form of Jesus' death, that is, *death by capital sentence at the hands of the Roman authorities.*

In the theory now being proposed, Paul only gradually came to the insight that he himself, after all of his long missionary journeys, after all of his faithful witness and service on behalf of Jesus, his Lord, now might be asked to embrace a form of death like that Jesus experienced. Paul had long reflected on the humiliation of "Christ crucified." Yet conceivably it was only during his own extended Roman imprisonment that he began to reflect explicitly on the nature of the Roman verdict against Jesus and the Roman implementation of that verdict.[2]

In the theory now being proposed, Paul gradually came to recognize that the Roman authorities' estimation of him could turn out to be comparable to their earlier estimation of Jesus, Paul's Lord. And, if such could be the authorities' estimation of Paul, might it not also be their estimation of other disciples who manifested a similar allegiance to Jesus as Lord. In writing, Paul thus wanted to acclimate his readers to the "scandal" of a second Roman death verdict.[3] He also wanted to acclimate them to the idea that all Philippian Christians with a committed allegiance to Jesus as Lord might, depending upon events, find themselves giving testimony in circumstances similar to Paul's, that is, before Roman authorities.

As the analysis of the preceding four passages has established, Paul's perspective regarding the Roman authorities in Philippians is manifestly different from his perspective in Romans 13:1–7. To be sure, Paul does not oppose Roman rule in the manner of the Zealots. Nor does he suggest any alternative to the empire that the Roman authorities have established. Nevertheless, he steadfastly insists on the unsurpassed sovereignty of Jesus and pointedly locates every human entity in subjection to Jesus. Earthly practices and earthly citizenship, Roman citizenship included, are to be judged against the standards of heavenly citizenship. Further, an integral feature of Christian discipleship is "standing firm" against the idolatrous claims and blandishments of those human authorities who are headed for destruction.

COLOSSIANS, EPHESIANS, AND 2 TIMOTHY

In the perspective of the present study, the fact that Colossians, Ephesians, and 2 Timothy all image Paul in chains is significant in and of itself fully apart from the question of whether any of these letters was actually authored by Paul.[4] Even if all three were written by associates or disciples of Paul, these letters vividly portray Paul reacting to the circumstances of his chained custody. Further, inasmuch as each of these letters reflects a situation of *extended* custody, imprisonment by the Roman authorities must be presumed as a dimension of each letter's *Paulusbild*. In other words, in each letter Paul is a *Roman* prisoner.

From an analysis of each letter's contents, what can be gleaned relative to the place of imprisonment? While there is nothing in Colossians and Ephesians to specify the location where Paul is being held prisoner, 2 Timothy 1:17 expressly portrays Rome as his place of custody. Other references in 2 Timothy suggest that Paul's judicial process is nearing a decisive verdict. Paul has had a "first defense" at which his possible supporters all deserted him (4:16). Indeed, he is at "the point of being sacrificed" (4:8). Nevertheless, an interval of judicial respite is indicated by Paul's desire that Timothy travel to his side bringing Paul's books and parchments (4:13).

Colossians. In Colossians, the identity of Paul as a prisoner in chains is presented only at the end of the letter. Colossians 4:3 first discloses that he is chained. In 4:18, the final verse of the letter, Paul dramatically petitions that his readers "remember my chains." Both of these references take on fuller meaning when they are viewed in the context of Paul's words in other parts of the letter.

In 1:24 Paul memorably relates his own suffering to Christ's afflictions and indicates that Paul's present sufferings benefit his readers. At this point in the letter, the nature of Paul's suffering is not explained. Only when this verse is read in light of Paul's references to his chains in 4:3 and 4:18 does it become apparent that chained confinement is a central element in the suffering that Paul alludes to.

In 4:3–4 Paul asks his readers to pray for him in his chains in order that a door will be opened for the proclamation that has been entrusted to him. What is being imaged here should be emphasized: Paul, who is in chains for "the mystery of Christ," asks prayers that he may be strengthened. Clearly, there is an added dimension to such a supplication when it comes from someone who is bound and imprisoned. Is it via this verse that the letter's readers learn for the first time that Paul writes from Roman custody? Or are the recipients of the letter already well aware of Paul's controversial circumstances?

If 4:3–4 makes a significant impact on Paul's readers and if the reference in 4:10 to Aristarchus as Paul's "fellow prisoner" contributes to this impact, 4:18, the final verse of the letter dramatically completes a rhetorical strategy whose centerpiece is Paul's chains. In order to appreciate the relationship between its major components, it is useful to consider this verse first in its totality with its key sentence emphasized: "I, Paul, write this greeting with my own hand. *Remember my chains.* Grace be with you."

If the key middle sentence had been omitted, v. 18 would convey a conventional greeting by an apostle written in his own hand. In effect, it is the middle sentence that provides this verse with its incandescent meaning. Before proceeding to a detailed exegesis of Paul's entreaty, it is useful to ask whether Paul is to be imagined writing these words while bound with a set of hand chains or

manacles. (There is surely a contrast between the situation portrayed here and the situation imaged when Paul takes the pen into
his own hands in 1 Cor. 16:21.) Seemingly, there is a special
poignancy to Paul's "desire" to write the letter's conclusion himself. He is still striving to carry out the "formalities" of letter writing despite the fact that he is now in chains.

In the Pauline corpus there is scarcely another exhortation that
so effectively communicates Paul's circumstances, his hopes, and
his commitment as this simple three-word exhortation of Colossians: "Remember my chains." These words vividly position Paul
in his readers' minds as bound with chains. How precisely is Paul
bound? With feet and hand chains? With full body chains whose
weight impedes him from walking? Is he chained to one or more
soldiers? It is left to the readers of the letter to envision Paul's
exact circumstances. However they image the concrete details of
his chains, what is unmistakable to them is that Paul now writes
as a bound Roman prisoner.

This same sentence, especially in conjunction with 1:24 and 4:3,
underscores Paul's faithfulness. Paul is in chains not for any scandalous reason but rather for the sake of Christ's body, including the
Christians of Colossae. Seemingly, Paul has worn these chains for
a considerable time. There is nothing in Colossians to suggest that
Paul's release is imminent. They are now the insignia of his faithfulness, and he asks that he be remembered and prayed for as he
continues to wear them.

Finally, is there not a dimension in the meaning of this sentence
that expresses a visceral resentment of his bonds and his custody?
Paul has a degree of freedom. Colossians 4:7–14 indicates that he
has a circle of friends around him and that he has the assistance of
a secretary to assist him in writing this letter. Nevertheless, is
there not a note of weariness in this cry from Paul's heart? Is there
not the sense that, in asking to have his chains remembered, Paul
is also expressing his desire to be freed from them?

Ephesians. In assessing Ephesians as a prison letter, its significant similarities to and differences from Colossians should be
noted at the outset even if space limitations preclude a full comparison. There is a verbal identity between phrases at the closing

of both letters; also both letters are to be brought to their respective destinations by the same person, Tychicus. But the universality of Ephesians distinguishes it from Colossians, which has the format of a letter to a specific community. Ephesians is also more doctrinal in its contents, and its initial chapters are characterized by a remarkable serenity.

Notwithstanding the serene quality present in its opening chapters, the *Paulusbild* that gradually emerges in this letter is that of a prisoner in chains and indeed a prisoner who asks prayers that he may boldly proclaim the gospel that has been entrusted to him. There are nuances in the Greek that indicate the forcefulness with which Paul's appeal is made at critical junctures in chapters 3 and 4. Nevertheless, the following passages demonstrate that, in writing to Gentiles, Paul dramatically postulates the connection between his audience and his own chains:

> For this reason I, Paul, a prisoner for Christ Jesus on behalf of you Gentiles . . . (3:1)

> So I ask you not to lose heart over what I am suffering for you, which is your glory. (3:13)

> I therefore, a prisoner for the Lord, beg you to lead a life worthy of the calling to which you have been called. (4:1)

These references to Paul's custody are complemented and intensified by the final image of Paul that Ephesians imparts. In a manner similar to Colossians, Ephesians asks its readers to keep Paul's chains fixed in their memories. The powerful, paradoxical way in which this is done is through the image of "an ambassador in a chain."

> To that end keep alert with all perseverance, making supplication for all the saints, and also for me, that utterance may be given me in opening my mouth *boldly* to proclaim the mystery of the gospel, for which I am *an ambassador in a chain;* that I may declare it *boldly,* as I ought to speak. (6:18b–20; emphasis added)

In the imperial world in which the readers of Ephesians lived, the role of the ambassador was well understood. Within this Roman world, appointment as an ambassador ranked among the highest possible appointments. Ambassadors were chosen for their recognized reliability for speaking and acting on behalf of Rome's interests. They were, in effect, buttressed by and protected by the power of Rome. Their rights and privileges were accordingly duly recognized.

In this context, Paul's description of himself as "an ambassador in a chain" could not have failed to arrest the imaginations of readers in Ephesus and indeed anywhere in the empire. Paul was the ambassador of his Lord, chosen for a mission that presumed his reliability and entrusted with a profound message. However, instead of being received with high protocol, he was received into chained imprisonment. Nevertheless, he remained steadfastly committed to proclaiming the gospel entrusted to him. Desirous of making this proclamation with proper *boldness* (he mentions his responsibility to testify "with boldness" twice in the passage just cited), Paul asks to be supported through prayer.

What a memorable closing appeal! What disciple, knowing of Paul's great faithfulness in Christ's service, would not want to respond generously to Paul's request for prayers to strengthen him for continued bold proclamation? And what disciple, well familiar with the realities of Roman power and the prestige of Rome's ambassadors, would not be startled by the knowledge that the power of Rome was now being used to keep Paul, Christ's ambassador(!), in *Roman* chains?

2 Timothy. This letter contains a remarkable number of references to Paul's judicial circumstances and his attitude toward his confinement and possible death. 2 Timothy unmistakably identifies Rome as the site of Paul's imprisonment (1:17) and also indicates that a decisive verdict is still in the offing. Paul reflects in 4:8 that he is at "the point of being sacrificed." In 4:16 he laments that at his "first defense," his potential supporters all deserted him. Nevertheless, an interval of judicial respite is indicated by Paul's desire that Timothy travel to his side bringing Paul's books and parchments (4:13). Paul presumably is able to use these items. Since Paul's situation is severe enough that it involves the shadow of a death verdict, but is also liberal enough to allow for visitors, books, and writing materials, it is possible to conjecture that he is in a situation of "military custody." Further, he is being guarded at a somewhat out-of-the-way setting within the boundaries of Rome (2 Tim. 1:17).

The scandal occasioned by Paul's chains is referred to in 2 Timothy in a way done in no other letter. The author of the letter had various purposes in writing (for example, in 2:18, those propagating a false teaching regarding the resurrection are attacked). However, the contrast between those who are unashamedly faithful to Paul and those who now prove unreliable is surely one of 2 Timothy's central themes. The following passages show that Paul is preoccupied with the contrasting responses that his status as a chained prisoner has elicited:

> Do not be ashamed then of testifying to our Lord, nor of me his prisoner, but share in suffering for the gospel in the power of God. (1:8)

> You are aware that all who are in Asia turned away from me and among them Phygelus and Hermogenes. (1:15)

> May the Lord grant mercy to the household of Onesiphorus, for he often refreshed me; he was not ashamed of my chains, but when he arrived in Rome he searched for me eagerly and found me. (1:16–17)

> For Demas, in love with this present world, has deserted me and gone to Thessalonica. (4:10)

> At my first defense no one took my part; all deserted me. May it not be charged against them! (4:16)

It is also significant that 2 Timothy portrays Paul himself as refusing to be shamed by what he has experienced: "For this Gospel I was appointed a preacher and apostle and teacher, and therefore I suffer as I do. *But I am not ashamed,* for I know whom I have believed, and I am sure that he is able to guard until that Day what has been entrusted to me" (1:11–12). Paul is resentful over the fact that he continues to be kept chained "like a criminal" (2:9), but he refuses to regard his chains as a badge of dishonor.

The political and judicial terminology in 2 Timothy is noteworthy. The locus of the letter is the imperial capital, the seat of the empire's supreme tribunal, and the residence of emperors who style themselves (and are styled) as "lords" and "saviors." Additionally it should be noted that the arrival of the emperor, complete with retinue, for official ceremonies and events is classically referred to as an "appearing" or as an "epiphany" (*epiphaneia*). Given this context, it is significant that the term *epiphaneia* occurs three times in this letter (1:10; 4:1; 4:8). Nevertheless, the "appearing" that 2 Timothy is concerned with is not that of the emperor but rather that of Jesus, who is truly *Savior* (1:10) and *Lord* (4:8). Paul is convinced that Jesus, his Lord, will *ultimately* save him because Jesus has already rescued Paul "from the lion's mouth" (4:17b–18).

What is more, it is Jesus who will provide Paul with final vindication. Paul first avows that Jesus has the power to judge both the living and the dead (4:1), an affirmation that presumably places Paul's Roman judges under Jesus' judgment. Paul then characterizes Jesus as "the righteous judge." This latter reference is contained in a memorable passage. Paul has just lyrically written that he has fought the good fight, finished the race, and kept the faith. What now awaits this faithful prisoner who is undaunted by his chains? A "crown of righteousness" awaits him that will be given him by an unsurpassed judge who judges with decisive probity: "Henceforth there is laid up for me the crown of righteousness, which the Lord, the righteous judge, will award to me on that Day, and not only to me but also to all who have loved his appearing" (4:8).

THE PERSPECTIVE OF PAUL, A CHAINED PRISONER IN ROME

The first objective of this brief section is to treat the fully unexpected developments that occurred in Paul's journey after he wrote Romans 13:1–7 to the Christians at Rome. The second objective is to underscore the "revisionism" of Philippians vis-à-vis the counsels of Romans 13.

The Acts of the Apostles, 2 Timothy, and Philippians—three distinct texts within the New Testament canon—are in fundamental agreement that Paul came to Rome not as a missionary bound for Spain but rather as a prisoner in chains. What can be gleaned from these three documents regarding the attitude of this prisoner toward the Roman authorities and their imperial system?

As previously discussed, the Acts of the Apostles and 2 Timothy both depict Paul's faithfulness to Jesus, his Lord, within the capital of the Roman lord emperor. However, it is Philippians that is decisive for determining whether any shift took place in Paul's perspective since the time when he originally wrote so magisterially to the Christians of Rome. A close analysis of Philippians reveals that a dramatic shift did indeed occur in Paul's perspective. The Paul who authored Philippians as a chained prisoner in Rome effectively set aside the premises and the counsels he had earlier expressed in Romans 13:1–7.

In summary, Philippians, Acts, and 2 Timothy provide converging reports relative to Paul's situation of chained imprisonment in Rome. In the providence of Jesus, Paul's Lord, this custody proved to be the occasion for a replacement of the counsel that Paul had provided to the Roman Christians at an earlier stage of his journey.[5] As will be seen in chapter 9, this superseding of Romans 13:1–7 by Philippians has major consequences for the overall assessment of Christian attitudes toward Roman power within the New Testament writings.

NOTES

1. The analysis presented in this chapter represents a summary of five chapters from my forthcoming study, *Paul in Chains: The Impact of Roman Imprisonment in the Letters of Paul* (New York: Crossroad, 2001). Since the documentation for that study is too lengthy to include here, the notes for this chapter are restricted to a minimal number of clarifications and amplifications related to key positions taken in *Paul in Chains*.

2. During the time of his imprisonment, Paul came to view the cross (always a central element in his theology) through the lens of the *perpetration* of the cross. In other words, Paul's meditation on the actions of the Roman authorities in crucifying Jesus increased as the possibility of his own death by decree of the Roman authorities loomed larger.

3. With memorable eloquence Paul referred to the cross as "a scandal" in 1 Corinthians 1:23 and Galatians 5:11, and certainly one of Paul's principal objectives throughout his ministry was to address and "overcome" the scandal of Jesus' crucifixion. Ironically, nearing the end of his ministry, Paul now strives to address and overcome the scandal of his own Roman imprisonment and possible Roman execution.

4. That each letter powerfully images Paul in chains has been a heretofore neglected factor in discussions concerning authorship. *If* disciples or associates of Paul wrote these letters under Paul's name, then such authors elected to take on the most controversial and scandalous elements of Paul's persona.

5. Assuming the validity of the present construction of Paul's journey, one cannot but marvel at two paradoxes that emerged as this journey unfolded: (a) Paul arriving in Rome not as a free-traveling apostle bound for Spain but rather as a chained prisoner and (b) Paul initially writing *to Rome* with a *highly favorable* perspective regarding the Roman authorities but later writing *from Rome* with a *decidedly less favorable* perspective.

8

Revelation and the
Destruction of Roman Power

THE CANONICAL NEW TESTAMENT'S final work, the book of
Revelation, is also the work that is most critical of Roman
power. Because of its complex imagery, Revelation presents particular challenges for the interpreter. It is characterized by
indictments and judgments against Rome, but these indictments
are frequently expressed in highly symbolic, obscure terms.

It is thus appropriate to begin this chapter with a section treating some of the literary characteristics of Revelation. The next
section will address the crucial topic of God's sovereignty. Within
the context of God's sovereign rule, Revelation's denunciations of
the Roman empire and its predictions regarding the destruction of
this empire will then be analyzed. The concluding section will
treat Revelation's counsels to its Christian readers and auditors.

THE LITERARY CHARACTERISTICS
OF REVELATION

Even though there are elements in the book that defy easy catego-
rization, Revelation can be located within the apocalyptic and the
prophetic literary genres.[1] Revelation may be viewed as prophetic
in the sense that the author is entrusted with a divine vision concerning judgment and salvation and is authorized to denounce the

evil powers wreaking havoc upon God's people (in 1:3 and 22:7, 18, 19, the author himself describes his work as prophecy). Revelation may be viewed as apocalyptic in the sense that God's intervention against the power of evil is cataclysmic and definitive: all evil is overcome; all good is upheld. Revelation is apocalyptic also in the sense that it utilizes many of the compositional techniques associated with apocalyptic writing, especially symbolism, numerology, and recapitulation.

An appreciation for the technique of recapitulation is particularly important for interpreting the presentation that the author makes in the body of his work from 4:1 to 22:5.[2] In its fundamental terms, the same scenario is reiterated or "recapitulated" seven times in the visions that make up these chapters. Each vision opens with a section delineating God's sovereignty. The role of evil is then specified, and God's intervention against evil and in support of the faithful is announced. The repetition of this general pattern does admit of considerable variation, however. While each vision expresses the basic pattern, it does so in a distinctive fashion. Thus, for example, the predictions of the Roman empire's end that occur in chapters 14, 16, 17, 18, and 19 are expressed in significantly different terms even though the fundamental schema of God destroying evil and vindicating the faithful underlies all of them.

Further, the judgments announced against the empire are grounded in the foundational judgment that is being announced against Satan. In the vivid presentation of Revelation 13:4, the Roman empire is imaged as the agent of Satan in this world! Here we may recall the memorable words attributed to Satan in Luke 4:4–6, where Satan avows that the authority and glory of "all the kingdoms of the world" have been delivered to him.

Who authored Revelation and to whom was it addressed?[3] In 1:1 the author gives his name as John and indicates that he is a servant of Jesus Christ who has had a revelation from Jesus entrusted to him. In 1:9 John further identifies himself as someone who is a brother to his readers and one who shares with them "the tribulation, and the kingdom and the patient endurance." He also relates that he has received these visions on the island of Patmos where he is located "on account of the word of God and the testimony of Jesus."

The designated recipients of John's word are Christians belonging to churches in seven cities within the Roman province of Asia.[4] Before proceeding to the body of his work (seven visions each of which delineates God's sovereign judgment), John addresses a distinct prophetic message to each of the seven churches. In presenting his text in this way, the author seems to envision that his work will travel as a kind of circular letter among these churches. Besides being instructed by the message specifically intended for them, members of a given church could draw insights from the specific messages addressed to six sister churches. In addition, every member of John's audience would receive guidance and encouragement from the last nineteen chapters of the book.

What is the political context for John's prophecies? In what years did John compose his work? Neither of these questions can be answered precisely, but it is useful to speculate regarding several of the factors that are relevant to each question. It is distinctly possible that John was banished to Patmos by order of the Roman authorities. He writes that he is there "on account of the word of God and the testimony of Jesus." He has also indicated to his readers that he shares "the tribulation" with them. If Roman-imposed exile is indeed John's situation, then Revelation should be understood as a type of "underground literature" that may have been subject to confiscation by the Roman authorities who mandated John's exile. On this reading, Roman censorship supplies an additional rationale for the obliqueness and the complexity of John's repeated references to the demise of the Roman empire.

Several passages in Revelation indicate that a significant number of Christians have already suffered martyrdom by the time that John writes (see especially 6:9–11; 16:6; 17:6; 18:24; 20:4; see also the treatment of martyrdom below). John's manner of presentation reflects his personal distress over the fact that the cavalier and wanton shedding of the blood of these martyrs has not yet been requited. However, there is nothing in his text to suggest that widespread persecution was occurring at the actual time that John wrote. A principal concern is rather with the devastating persecution that appears to loom in the not distant future (2:10; 3:10). Indeed, one of John's objectives is to strengthen his Christian readers in the "patient endurance" that they will need in order to withstand and surmount this persecution.

It is not possible to establish the date of Revelation precisely, but several factors seem to point to the years and decades after A.D. 64, the year in which Nero, according to the report of Tacitus, scapegoated and brutally persecuted a group of Christians in Rome.[5] It will be seen below that John evidences a strong revulsion for the Roman empire, its authorities, and its practices. The present objective is to assess known events that could have engendered this revulsion in John. Could any Christian writer have arrived at such a thoroughgoing disdain for Roman rule prior to the regime of Nero?

It is also possible that the destruction of the Jerusalem temple by the Roman forces in A.D. 70 might have significantly influenced John. On this reading, John, an author who was well familiar with the writings of Jeremiah, Ezekiel, and Isaiah,[6] recognized that Rome had replicated the destruction of the temple that imperial Babylon had accomplished in 587 B.C. in conjunction with the exile of the Jerusalem populace. In several places John refers to Rome under the code name "Babylon the Great." He was influenced to use this term not only because of his knowledge that the Babylonian empire had crashed so suddenly and so dramatically; it was even more appropriate since Rome had reenacted the deed for which Babylon was most infamous.[7]

Finally, the abuses associated with Domitian might also have galvanized John to produce a work that is so hostile to the Roman empire, its authorities, and its practices. Pliny's letter to the emperor Trajan seems to assume that trials of Christians were held during the reign of Domitian.[8] (Is the martyrdom of Antipas at Pergamum that is mentioned in 2:13 to be situated during the reign of Domitian or earlier?) Further, Domitian, as recklessly as Nero, attempted to secure his position by means of self-deifying titles. A classic instance of Domitian's penchant for such self-aggrandizement was his demand for the title "lord and god."[9] Archaeological evidence for the establishment of Domitian's cult in the province of Asia includes the enormous statue of him that was constructed at the temple dedicated to him at Ephesus. Cumulatively, such developments as these would have been egregiously affronting to a disciple of Jesus with John's sensibilities and convictions.

The approach of the present study is to connect Revelation's date of composition with the affronting and scandalous events that occurred within the Roman empire in the second half of the first Christian century. The perspective of Revelation is so decisively anti-Roman that episodes that John considered particularly outrageous must have occurred prior to his composition of this work. Was Nero's brutal persecution sufficient to spur John to write? Was the destruction of the Jerusalem temple a horrendous deed that contributed further to his outrage? Or was it the case that John did not write until the excesses and the aberrations of Domitian had been added to these preceding developments and to others besides?

THE SOVEREIGNTY OF GOD AND THE LAMB

Whatever John's degree of familiarity with the imperial ruler cult that flourished especially under such emperors as Nero and Domitian, it is unmistakable that Revelation affirms the full and complete sovereignty of God and Jesus, portrayed as the Lamb who was slain. Fundamentally, Revelation is concerned with God's sovereignty and with the worship that is due to God and to the Lamb *alone.* The heavenly throne room is repeatedly portrayed in majestic terms, and it is made clear that, from their thrones, God and the Lamb exercise ultimate power over Satan and over every entity upon the earth, rulers and kings in particular.[10]

References to heaven and God's sovereignty occur at the outset of each of the seven visions that comprise the body of Revelation[11] and also at other junctures. The following passage elucidates the grandness with which Revelation's heavenly hosts acclaim the majesty of God and the Lamb:

> Worthy art thou, our Lord and God, to receive glory and honor and power, for thou didst create all things, and by thy will they existed and were created. (4:11)

In the second passage to be considered, the praise of God and the Lamb is even more majestic and encompassing. John first hears the acclaim of the hosts of heaven, but the voices of all other creatures are then added to the heavenly chorus:

> Then I looked, and I heard around the throne and the living creatures and the elders the voice of many angels, numbering myriads of

myriads and thousands of thousands, saying with a loud voice, "Worthy is the Lamb who was slain, to receive power and wealth and wisdom and might and honor and glory and blessing!" And I heard every creature in heaven and on earth and under the earth and in the sea, and all therein, saying, "To him who sits upon the throne and to the Lamb be blessing and honor and glory and might for ever and ever!" (5:11–13)

Other passages attesting to the unsurpassed sovereignty of God and Christ could be cited (e.g., 1:5 and 17:14), but it suffices to present only one additional passage. In the passage that follows, the arrival of a celestial rider who is the Word of God is announced. The other titles that are here attributed to Christ establish that his status and power incomparably surpass those of any earthly ruler.[12] It will be seen below that this heavenly rider and an accompanying angel decisively conquer and punish the leaders and allies of Rome. John's description of Christ in this passage is as follows:

Then I saw heaven opened, and behold, a white horse! He who sat upon it is called Faithful and True, and in righteousness he judges and makes war. His eyes are like a flame of fire, and on his head are many diadems; and he has a name inscribed which no one knows but himself. He is clad in a robe dipped in blood, and the name by which he is called is The Word of God. And the armies of heaven, arrayed in fine linen, white and pure, followed him on white horses. From his mouth issues a sharp sword with which to smite the nations, and he will rule them with a rod of iron; he will tread the wine press of the fury of the wrath of God the Almighty. On his robe and on his thigh he has a name inscribed, King of kings and Lord of lords. (19:11–16)

REVELATION'S COMPREHENSIVE INDICTMENT OF IMPERIAL ROME

Chapter 2 delineated the various mechanisms by which the Roman authorities conquered and administered a vast empire. The present section will disclose that John, the author of Revelation, did not stand in awe of Roman power. On the contrary, Revelation makes a thoroughgoing indictment of Roman power and predicts its demise.

Before considering the manner in which Revelation indicates the judgment and the destruction of the Roman empire, it is useful to reflect for a moment regarding the boldness of John's endeavor. Apocalyptic and prophetic writing typically proclaims that God's judgment will be decisively visited upon the evil regime of the given moment. As noted above, Revelation stands within the literary categories of prophetic and apocalyptic. Nevertheless, within these notably vivid forms of writing, Revelation's attack on Roman power is still breathtaking in its conceptualization and in its literary accomplishment.

Recall that John is located in a setting in which Roman power is firmly established and the Roman system is flourishing. Local elites in Ephesus and in other provincial cities of Asia have enthusiastically accepted the Roman system and are actively advancing the cult of Rome's emperors. Roman-authorized commerce is profitable, and Roman propaganda concerning "peace and order" and Rome's invincibility and eternity is extensive. In this daunting context, John conceives of Revelation, commits it to writing, and takes steps to circulate it.

John first devises coded reference terms for the various features of the Roman imperial order. He then employs recapitulation to hammer home the point of Rome's fundamental perversity while incrementally extending the bill of particulars against the empire. The same device of recapitulation allows him to announce the destruction of Rome repeatedly while suggesting a variety of mechanisms by which this destruction will be accomplished.[13] Finally, by unmistakably affirming the link between Roman power and Satan's deceptions, John is able to forecast that the decisive destruction of Rome will be an almost effortless endeavor for the sovereign God and the sovereign Lamb, who have already acted decisively against Satan.

In the first part of chapter 13 and elsewhere, the image of the beast from the sea stands for Rome and its imperial power.[14] In the second half of chapter 13, "the beast from the earth" also stands for aspects of Roman imperial power, perhaps especially the local elites who participate in this power and promote it. (In 16:13 and 19:20, the figure of "the false prophet" is equivalent to the figure of the second beast.) Imperial Rome is referred to also under the figure of "Babylon the Great" (14:8; 16:9; 17:5; 18:2ff.). The Roman empire is also imaged as "the great harlot" (17:1ff.; 19:2) and as "the great city" (16:19; in 11:8, "the city" that is referred to is probably a blend of Jerusalem and Rome). In the first of the seven visions comprising the body of the book, the Roman empire is identified not by any of these terms but rather by a catalogue of its personnel ranging from the "kings of the earth" and "generals" to the slaves[15] who serve in imperial administration (6:15).

At times, these various images merge with one another and are integrated into unfolding scenarios that are difficult for the reader to decipher. Painting with brush strokes that are rich in symbolism, John does not systematically distinguish among the following entities: the Roman empire, Roman imperial power, the city of Rome, and the power of others in alliance with Rome. An especially noteworthy instance of John's capacity to merge various images for imperial Rome in an arresting manner occurs in 17:17, where it is affirmed that the beast (an image of Roman imperial power) will hate the harlot (an image of the Roman empire) and destroy her with fire. In this instance what John's vision seems to suggest is that destruction will be visited upon the Roman empire through internal conflict.

What are the abuses for which God and the Lamb will bring the empire to destruction? Again, each of seven visions insists on Rome's fundamental perversity while focusing upon particular abuses. It suffices to provide a general sense of the indictments that John is setting forth. John's basic objections to Roman practice can be considered under five headings.

1. Rome's martyrdom of Jesus' disciples certainly heads John's list. As previously noted, there is no indication of official persecution as John writes. Nevertheless, John righteously castigates imperial Rome for the deaths that have already occurred. Four passages in Revelation in which the *blood* of martyrs is vividly portrayed serve to establish John's basic perspective. In the first memorable passage, the slain martyrs themselves call out for vengeance:

> When he opened the fifth seal, I saw under the altar the souls of those who had been slain for the word of God and for the witness

they had borne; they cried out with a loud voice, "O Sovereign Lord, holy and true, how long before thou wilt judge and avenge our blood on those who dwell upon the earth?" (6:9–10)

In the denunciations of Roman power that appear in chapters 16 and 17, the martyrs' blood is also vividly portrayed. In 16:6, after the third bowl poured by the angel turns rivers and fountains into blood, the angel relates how fitting a punishment this is: "For men have shed the blood of saints and prophets, and thou has given them blood to drink." In 17:6, when the seer first sees the vision of the great harlot, a vital part of the image of her abandon is that this harlot is drunk with the blood of Jesus' disciples: "And I saw the woman drunk with the blood of the saints and the blood of the martyrs of Jesus."

2. The fourth passage in which the blood of the martyrs is mentioned also contains a reference to the blood of "all who have been slain on earth." This indictment of imperial Rome thus adds a second entry into John's bill of particulars. John is highly affected by the slaying of Jesus' disciples. He is also influenced by the other deaths for which Roman power is responsible: "And in her was found the blood of prophets and of saints, *and of all who have been slain on earth*" (18:24).

3. The third category of Roman abuse that John critiques in Revelation is the category of blasphemy and idolatry. This broad category encompasses a multitude of imperial Rome's abuses that can be treated only cursorily here. The blasphemous claims made by Roman emperors and their provincial clients are central to what John castigates in numerous passages involving the two beasts. In 13:1 John sees a beast with ten horns and seven heads "and a *blasphemous* name upon its heads." In 13:5-6 John states that this first beast was given "a mouth for uttering haughty and *blasphemous* words" and that it opened its mouth "to utter *blasphemies* against God, *blaspheming* his name and his dwelling."

In addition to decrying blasphemy, John also decries the success that those who cooperate with Rome at the provincial level have had in promoting the worship of Rome and its emperors. In lamenting the work of the second beast, John states:

[The second beast] makes the earth and its inhabitants worship the first beast whose mortal wound was healed. It works great signs, even making fire come down from heaven to earth in the sight of men; and by the signs which it is allowed to work in the presence of the beast, it deceives those who dwell on earth, bidding them make an image for the beast which was wounded by the sword and yet lived. (13:12b–14)

In John's schema, the invincibility and the eternity of imperial Rome are closely related to the other aspects of Rome's idolatry. In 13:4 John laments the seeming success that has been achieved by this propaganda: "and they worshiped the beast, saying 'Who is like the beast and who can fight against it?'" Rome's propaganda regarding eternity is also in evidence in 18:7b, where the great harlot brazenly claims: "a queen I sit, I am no widow, mourning I shall never see."

4. Economic exploitation is the fourth significant charge that John proffers against Rome. In conjunction with the critique of idolatry, Revelation 13:6 protests against the licenses that Rome has mandated as a requirement for all economic transactions. John subsequently devotes the whole of Revelation 18 to a criticism of the "wantonness" that drives Rome's economic activity. John recognizes that the client kings, merchants, and shipowners who participated in Rome's commercial network gained prosperity. They mourn her demise for this reason. Nevertheless, it is John's view that Rome has enriched her clients *only* because she herself has become immersed in extravagance, luxury, and indulgence.

John does not explicitly claim that Rome's prosperity involves the exploitation of the provinces she has conquered, but Revelation 18 approaches such a claim.[16] Significantly, John's catalogue of the luxury items that Rome voraciously consumes ends with "slaves, that is, human souls" (18:13b). Rome's "consumption" of slaves is thus a contemptible feature of the socioeconomic patterns that John recognizes and deplores.

5. John's fifth rationale for indicting imperial Rome is fundamental to all of the preceding indictments. For, as indicated at the outset of this chapter, Revelation's grounding premise is that

Rome is *demonic;* that is, its power has fundamentally been derived from Satan. In 12:9 Michael and his angels cast the great dragon, "Satan, the deceiver of the whole world," down to earth. This event is indeed catastrophic for humankind: "But woe to you, O earth and sea, for the devil has come down to you in great wrath, because he knows that his time is short!" (12:12).

Failing in his attempt to destroy the woman and child with whom it is in cosmic conflict (12:13–17), the dragon (Satan) then enters into alliance with a horrific beast (imperial Rome) rising from the sea. In 13:2b and then in 13:4 John explicitly indicates the source of the beast's power and the continuing relationship between the dragon and the beast:

> And to it [the beast] the dragon gave his power and his throne and great authority. (13:2b)

> Men worshiped the dragon, for he had given his authority to the beast, and they worshiped the beast, saying, "Who is like the beast, and who can fight against it?" (13:4)

REVELATION'S PROPHECY OF ROME'S DEMISE

Revelation prophesies the violent destruction of imperial Rome so frequently and so emphatically that it is possible for the contemporary reader to become overly acclimated to the truly astonishing perspective that John is expressing. Remember that Revelation's predictions of Rome's destruction are not prophecy *ex eventu.* On the contrary, John's predictions concerning Roman destruction are made at a time when Roman power is at its zenith, at a time when the destruction of imperial Rome is scarcely imaginable.

Recall from chapter 2 above that, at the end of Augustus' reign, Rome's standing armies numbered approximately 300,000 legionaries, auxiliaries, and special cohorts. Recall the vast territories that the empire comprised and its total population of approximately 54,000,000, with perhaps 1,000,000 in the city of Rome. Recall the sophisticated system of provincial administration and provincial taxation that Augustus and his successors had achieved. According to Revelation, the entire apparatus of Roman rule will be destroyed.

The effectiveness of John's technique of recapitulation for announcing this astonishing prophecy should again be emphasized. In each of the seven visions in the body of Revelation, Rome's demise (including the related demise of Satan) is indicated. In the preceding section it was observed that different *reasons* for this destruction are given in the different visions. Similarly, there are different *mechanisms* for this destruction identified within the seven visions.

It is not feasible here to attempt an exhaustive treatment of every passage in Revelation that pertains to Rome's destruction. Instead, eight of the mechanisms for this destruction will be identified, and two of the final passages that describe Rome's downfall will be cited in full. Because they portray Rome's downfall with noteworthy vividness and because they occur near the end of John's work, these latter two passages can be regarded as the culmination of John's prophecies of destruction.

A central point is that in all of the mechanisms for Rome's downfall, the hand of God is seen. In other words, every calamity that befalls Rome is divinely initiated and is in some sense a divine response to the abuses that Rome has perpetrated. A list of the mechanisms for Rome's destruction is as follows: by earthquake (6:12; 8:13; 11:13; 16:18); by fire (17:16; 18:8); through internal conflict (17:16); by pestilence and famine (18:8); by unspecified massacre (14:20); through unspecified violence (18:21); by Christ at the head of a heavenly army (17:14; 19:19-20). It should also be noted that unspecified divine power definitively consigns Satan in 20:10 to the lake of fire and sulphur.

That each of John's repeated predictions of Rome's destruction is made in vivid terms is shown by the passages that will now be considered in greater detail. Another salient feature of both of these passages as well as of the other passages of destruction is that John betrays no hint of remorse for the events that are unfolding. This outcome of Rome's destruction is, in John's view, well deserved.

"Fallen, fallen is Babylon the Great!" This ringing declaration, reflective of Isaiah 21:9, appears in Revelation 14:8 and again in 18:2.[17] As Revelation 18 continues, the unprecedented suddenness of Rome's fall is mentioned in 18:10, 17, and 19: "In one hour she has been laid waste." The following passage then describes the completeness of the destruction and explains why it was called for:

> Then a mighty angel took up a stone like a great millstone and threw it into the sea, saying, "So shall Babylon, the great city, be thrown down with violence, and shall be found no more; and the sound of harpers and minstrels, of flute players and trumpeters, shall be heard in thee no more; and a craftsman of any craft shall be found in thee no more; and the sound of the millstone shall be heard in thee no more; and the light of a lamp shall shine in thee no more and the voice of bridegroom and bride shall be heard in thee no more; for thy merchants were the great men of the earth, and all nations were deceived by thy sorcery. And in her was found the blood of prophets and of saints, and of all who have been slain on earth." (18: 21-24)

The analysis of the sovereignty of God and Christ that was made earlier in this chapter directed attention to the way in which Revelation 19 images Christ as a resplendent rider at the head of the armies of heaven. The excerpt from Revelation 19 that will now be considered continues the description of this scene delineating the harsh outcome that befalls imperial Rome and its allies.

The imagery that John here employs is arguably Revelation's most grotesque. In a harsh outcome the carcasses of those who had allied themselves with the beast and the false prophet serve as fare for the birds, who are summoned to participate at a sumptuous banquet. The fate of the beast and the false prophet is to be cast into the lake of fire and sulphur (in 20:10 Satan is consigned to this same lake). All facets of this routing of Rome's forces are effortlessly accomplished by divine intervention, expressly by the power of Christ's word, the sword that issues from his mouth. The carnage that is inflicted on Rome and its minions results without any battle actually being fought:

> Then I saw an angel standing in the sun, and with a loud voice he called to all the birds that fly in midheaven, "Come, gather for the great supper of God, to eat the flesh of kings, the flesh of captains, the flesh of mighty men, the flesh of horses and their riders, and the flesh of all men, both free and slave, both small and great." And I saw the beast and the kings of the earth with their armies gathered to make war against him who sits upon the horse and against his army.

And the beast was captured, and with it the false prophet, who in its presence had worked the signs by which he deceived those who had received the mark of the beast and those who worshiped its image. These two were thrown alive into the lake of fire that burns with sulphur. And the rest were slain by the sword of him who sits upon the horse, the sword that issues from his mouth; and all the birds were gorged with their flesh. (19:17–21)

ENCOURAGING CHRISTIANS FOR RESISTANCE AND MARTYRDOM

In Revelation 13 and 14, John solemnly appeals to his audience asking that they give a committed response to what they have heard and read. John's two solemn appeals are as follows:

Here is a call for the endurance and faith of the saints. (13:10c)

Here is a call for the endurance of the saints, those who keep the commandments of God and the faith of Jesus. (14:12)

The Greek word *hypomonē*, translated as "endurance" in these two passages, is a term that John favors. He uses it five times at the outset of his book to characterize the fundamental stance to which he and the Christians of the seven churches are called. It is also possible to translate *hypomonē* as "steadfast resistance" in an effort to indicate that John's intended meaning involves an active witness against Roman idolatry as well as an uncompromising faithfulness in times of actual persecution.[18] That John does envision Christian faithfulness involving a conscious withdrawal from idolatrous practices is corroborated at 18:4. Babylon the Great is under sentence of destruction and a heavenly voice instructs Christians as to the following line of conduct: "Come out of her, my people, lest you take part in her sins, lest you share in her plagues." The dimension of active disengagement thus seems integral to the counsel that John is providing to his readers.

As is evident from the analysis made in the preceding section of this chapter, Revelation repeatedly adverts to the existence of martyrs and to their vindication. It should be underscored that, even though no general persecution is occurring as he writes, John considers it a definite possibility that the Christians of his own day may face martyrdom. In the first vision of his book, John indicates that the vindication of those who have already been martyred is not yet at hand. The reason for this delay is that further martyrdom is in the offing. Thus, these first martyrs must rest "a little longer until the number of their fellow servants and their brethren should be complete, who were to be killed as they themselves had been" (6:11b). John's words to the Christians of Smyrna corroborate this point concerning the proximity of martyrdom:

> Do not fear what you are about to suffer. Behold, the devil is about to throw some of you into prison that you may be tested, and for ten days you will have tribulation. Be faithful unto death, and I will give you the crown of life. (2:10)

A feature of Revelation that is reminiscent of the stark alternatives of the Gospel of John is Revelation's sharp disjunction between allegiance to the name of imperial Rome and allegiance to the name of Jesus.[19] In Revelation 13, the role of the second beast (Rome's client rulers and priesthoods) is to promote worship of the first beast (imperial Rome), that is, to influence as many as possible to manifest allegiance to imperial Rome. In John's vivid presentation, the objective of the two beasts is to mark the name of the first beast on the maximum number of the populace. As previously noted, economic sanctions were one means of coercing this allegiance: "no one can buy or sell unless he has the mark, that is, *the name of the beast* or the number of its name" (13:17).

What precise concrete actions constitute giving allegiance and giving worship to the beast representing imperial Rome? Revelation nowhere specifies the concrete violations but presumably participating in any form of the imperial ruler cult and registering for imperial license to buy and sell lead the list of the practices that John seeks to prohibit. (A significant consideration is that Revelation speaks not a word regarding Roman taxation.) Whatever the identity of the specific practices that John intends to proscribe, his warning against accommodation is made in uncompromising terms. Any of John's audience engaging in such practices must know that they are placing their salvation in jeopardy by doing so. The following severe warning is delivered by an angel in Revelation 14:

> If any one worships the beast and its image, and receives a mark on his forehead or on his hand, he also shall drink the wine of God's wrath, poured unmixed into the cup of his anger, and he shall be tormented with fire and sulphur in the presence of the holy angels and in the presence of the Lamb. And the smoke of their torment goes up for ever and ever; and they have no rest, day or night, these worshipers of the beast and its image, and whoever receives *the mark of its name.* (14:9b-11)

The dire warning given in this passage should be correlated with perspectives expressed in several other passages in which John positively commends his readers for eschewing any participation in the worship of imperial Rome. Among the messages to the churches in Revelation 2 and 3, there are several instances in which churches are explicitly commended in terms of their faithfulness to the name of Jesus. The church at Philadelphia is so commended in the following terms: "you have kept my word and not denied my name" (3:8b). As a consequence, Jesus will protect this church during the great tribulation that is coming and will write three names (!) upon the faithful of this church: "the name of my God, and the name of the city of my God, . . . and my own new name" (3:12c).

The commendation that the church at Pergamum receives is even more auspicious, for the Christians at Pergamum have already faced martyrdom and have remained faithful: "you hold fast *my name* and you did not deny my faith even in the days of Antipas my witness, my faithful one who was killed among you" (2:13b).

John's messages to the seven churches also identify other abuses and dangers that do not directly relate to the idolatry of imperial Rome and its clients. Thus the approval given to the church at Ephesus for "enduring patiently and bearing up for my name's sake" (2:3) may be intended as an endorsement of faithful conduct in multiple areas. Regardless of the type of faithfulness that is being affirmed here, what is clear is that loyalty and honor to the name of Jesus are the standards for assessing the righteousness of all Christian conduct.

John also promotes a commitment to the name of Jesus in several of the majestic heavenly scenes that appear in the second half of Revelation. In each of these scenes Jesus' faithful are portrayed in circumstances of wondrous bliss. In each scene a principal feature distinguishing these disciples is the name that appears (or does not appear) on their foreheads.

The majestic figure of the Lamb appears auspiciously in two of these scenes. To reach the depth of John's meaning in these passages, it is important to recall that the worship of God and of the Lamb is the grounding reality for Revelation's critique of Roman power. The majesty of the heavenly worship before the throne of God and the Lamb, a phenomenon repeatedly described in Revelation, is the standard against which the counterfeit majesty of imperial Rome and its rulers is judged. The power of God and that of the Lamb will ultimately prevail throughout all of creation. The reality of this power and majesty is even now influential in the lives of the committed followers of the Lamb on earth.

But who is this Lamb who along with God possesses such power and majesty? Given the frequency with which John employs this image of the Lamb for Jesus in Revelation, it is clear that it possesses great meaning for him. How does John understand the meaning of the Lamb?[20] Revelation 5:6 and 5:12 provide the key to John's fascination with this image. In those verses the Lamb is fully described as "the Lamb who was slain." By whom was this Lamb slain? The simple placing of this question opens the way for a significant insight. John and his readers know that Jesus was slain by imperial Roman power. In the visions of John, this slain Lamb now stands in judgment of imperial Rome and possesses all power and complete sovereignty. It is precisely this Jesus so slain who now calls and encourages his own disciples vis-à-vis the slaying power of imperial Rome!

Consider now the majestic scene of the 144,000 who gather with the Lamb at the beginning of Revelation 14. What is the principal criterion by which this multitude gathers to sing a great song of praise before the heavenly throne? John tells his readers. These are the faithful followers of the Lamb "who had *his name* and *the Father's name* written on their foreheads" (14:1b).

In the dramatic judgment scene of Revelation 20, no reference is made to the Lamb, but there is obvious attention given to the insignia of those who have been faithful unto death. In this particular passage, the names that Jesus' faithful disciples do *not* have upon their foreheads is the point John emphasizes. John describes their appearance of these disciples and their future in the following terms:

> Also I saw the souls of those who had been beheaded for their testimony to Jesus and for the word of God, and who had not worshiped the beast or its image and had not received *its mark* on their foreheads or their hands. They came to life, and reigned with Christ a thousand years. (20:4b)

John's final encouragement to his readers to prove utterly faithful to the name of Jesus occurs within the vision closing the body of the book—in effect, the apex of his work. In the new heaven and the new earth that John now describes, the majesty of God and the Lamb prevail completely. It is to this ultimate reality that John again points his readers. Their bliss shall be complete and unending in the presence of God and the Lamb, and the credential for their joyous presence before the throne of God and the Lamb will be the name that they bear upon their foreheads:

> There shall no more be anything accursed, but the throne of God and of the Lamb shall be in it, and his servants shall worship him; they shall see his face, and *his name* shall be on their foreheads. And night shall be no more; they need not light of lamp or sun, for the Lord God will be their light, and they shall reign for ever and ever. (22:3–5)

NOTES

1. See R. Bauckham, *The Theology of the Book of Revelation* (Cambridge: Cambridge University Press, 1993), 2–17, for a discussion of Revelation as embodying the literary qualities of apocalypse, prophecy, and letter.

2. C. Talbert discusses various features of recapitulation, explaining that the seven visions of the end-time in Revelation all feature the same subject matter but with variations (*The Apocalypse* [Louisville, Ky.: Westminster John Knox, 1994], 7–8). Talbert perceptively observes that recapitulation allows an author to advance an argument by means of narrative. The repetition involved in recapitulation is necessary in order to ensure that the author's thesis "gets through."

3. See J. Roloff, *Revelation* (Minneapolis: Fortress, 1993), 8–12, for a discussion of the authorship of Revelation and its date of composition.

4. As discussed above in chapter 6, Revelation addresses readers who live within the Roman province of Asia. As noted in chapter 6 above, 1 Peter (in part) also addresses Christians living within this province.

5. See above, pp. 76–81, where 1 Peter's date and circumstances are discussed. That discussion is relevant for the present discussion of Revelation's date and circumstances. It is again useful to pose the question: Are these two documents written for the same generation of Asian Christians?

6. See F. Murphy, *Fallen Is Babylon* (Harrisburg, Pa.: Trinity Press International, 1998), 27–30, for a cogent discussion of John's rootedness in biblical literature even though there is not a single direct quotation of the Bible in Revelation.

7. The six references to "Babylon the Great" in Revelation (14:8; 16:19; 17:5; 18:2, 10, 21) stress Babylon's destruction and, as explicated below, Rome's destruction is one of John's principal themes. Nevertheless, the fact that Rome (like Babylon) destroyed Jerusalem and represented decadence may also have influenced John's use of this metaphor.

8. See R. Cassidy, *John's Gospel in New Perspective: Christology and the Realities of Roman Power* (Maryknoll, N.Y.: Orbis Books, 1992), 17–26, for an analysis of the situation that seems to be presumed in Pliny's letter to the emperor.

9. Ibid., 14–16.

10. Bauckham rightly insists on divine sovereignty and transcendence as foundational for all that is portrayed in Revelation (*Theology of the Book of Revelation*, 23–51). In Bauckham's view the entire critique of Roman power that is made in Revelation follows from the vision of the heavenly throne room and God's sovereign rule as these are described in Revelation 4.

11. See the outline of these seven visions that is presented by Talbert, *Apocalypse*, 12, who explicates how each of these seven visions opens with a scene in heaven.

12. See Roloff, *Revelation*, 217–20, for a nuanced analysis of the titles that are here attributed to Christ: "Word of God," "King of kings," and

"Lord of lords." Roloff comments that in John's perspective Christ is the *only* one who rightfully bears these names (p. 219).

13. As noted above, Talbert insightfully structures the body of Revelation in terms of seven visions (*Apocalypse*, 12). In Talbert's words, these seven visions recapitulate "the shift of the ages." The present interpretation adopts Talbert's schematization but emphasizes more than Talbert does that these visions generally and repeatedly critique Roman power. In other words, John's device of recapitulation enables him to denounce repeatedly the empire's abuses and to announce repeatedly the empire's demise.

14. In *Uneasy Neighbors: Christians and the State in the New Testament* (Minneapolis: Fortress, 1999), 151–61, W. Pilgrim provides an effective analysis of the way in which Revelation images Rome as "the beast," as "the great whore," and as "Babylon the great."

15. The presence of slaves among those facing retribution has long been a perplexing issue for commentators on Revelation, particularly in light of John's sympathetic reference to slaves in 18:13. However, if these "slaves" are understood as serving in various positions within the Roman emperor's administrative apparatus, then John's prediction is that they too are vulnerable, along with the kings, generals, and the rich.

16. See the valuable analysis of this chapter provided in R. Bauckham, "The Economic Critique of Rome in Revelation 18," in *The Climax of Prophecy* (Edinburgh: Clark, 1993), 338–83.

17. As indicated in n. 7 above, all six of John's references to Babylon stress its destruction.

18. See Pilgrim, *Uneasy Neighbors*, 165–75, for a helpful discussion of the meaning of *hypomonē* in terms of cultural resistance as well as endurance to martyrdom. Pilgrim rightly stresses (p. 174) that Revelation's "ethic of resistance" does not authorize hatred or violence.

19. The following paragraphs analyzing Revelation's disjunction between allegiance to the name of Jesus and allegiance to the name or "mark" of imperial Rome are influenced by my analysis of the "name" of Jesus as a source of life in John's Gospel and my consideration of Pliny's tactic of requiring that suspected Christians curse the name of Jesus. See my *John's Gospel in New Perspective*, 76–77 and 89–90.

20. Roloff provides a brief insightful excursus on the meaning of "the Lamb" as an image that John employs twenty-eight times within Revelation (*Revelation*, 78–79). In his analysis of this image, Roloff rightly stresses the meanings of sacrifice and dominion. In the perspective of the present study, the meaning that attaches to "the Lamb" (Jesus) as one slain by the power of imperial Rome is also extremely significant.

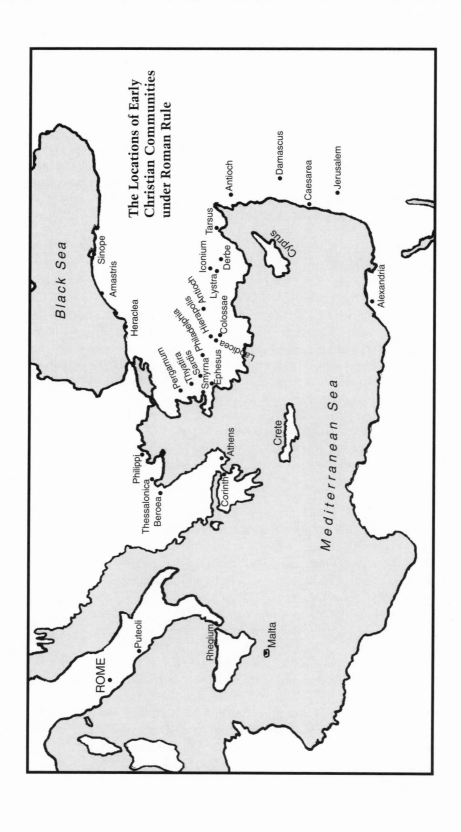

The Locations of Early
Christian Communities
under Roman Rule

Black Sea

Sinope

Amastris

Heraclea

Pergamum
Thyatira
Sardis
Smyrna
Ephesus
Philadelphia
Hierapolis
Antioch
Laodicea
Colossae
Iconium
Lystra
Derbe
Tarsus

Cyprus

Antioch

Damascus

Caesarea

Jerusalem

Alexandria

Mediterranean Sea

Crete

Athens

Corinth

Philippi
Thessalonica
Beroea

ROME

Puteoli

Rhegium

Malta

9

Overview of Christians and Roman Power in the New Testament Writings

A S A MEANS OF SUMMARIZING the principal findings of this study, this chapter's first two sections will conjecture regarding the instruction that second-century Christians would have derived from the New Testament writings considered above. The final section will discuss four ways in which conclusions reached in this study can contribute to the discipleship of Christians in the third millennium.

THE EXPECTATION OF PERSECUTION FROM THE ROMAN AUTHORITIES

Second-century Christians still lived within the context of the Roman empire. Their lives were still circumscribed by the decrees of emperors and governors. If the texts of the entire New Testament were in the possession of Christian communities in various cities of the Roman empire at some point in the second century, what key insights would these Christians have gained as they read, listened to, and reflected upon these writings?

A major thesis of this study is that the Christian communities would have found themselves repeatedly warned concerning trials, imprisonments, and martyrdom at the hands of the imperial authorities. These warnings and allusions occur in Luke's Gospel (and in the other Synoptics) and in John's Gospel. They are also extensively present within the Pauline corpus. Such warnings may also be present in 1 Peter. They are prominently and extensively set forth in Revelation. Although the Letter to the Hebrews has not been analyzed within this study, that work does refer to Roman persecution (10:32–39; 12:4).

In Luke 21:12–19, Jesus is portrayed specifically preparing his disciples to face trials before "kings and governors" and sentences of death for the sake of his name (similarly Mark 13:9–12 and Matt. 10:17–22). Luke also provides an extensive report of Jesus' own trial before Pilate and Herod Antipas, a trial that eventually resulted in the Roman governor's condemnation of Jesus to crucifixion. As discussed in chapter 4 above, John's Gospel portrays Jesus predicting Peter's martyrdom by Roman crucifixion (21:18–19). Jesus' words in 16:2b may also envision persecution by Roman officials who will execute Christians as a means of propitiating pagan gods.

Second-century readers of Acts would also have had transmitted to them reports of Jesus' disciples facing persecution and martyrdom at the hands of the Roman authorities. It must be recalled that various members of the Herod family functioned as delegates of Rome and thus exercised political power within the Roman system. A Roman official, Herod Agrippa I, executed the apostle James and arrested Peter with the same intention only to have his plan thwarted by divine intervention. According to Acts, Paul himself faced proceedings involving Roman officials in Philippi, Thessalonica, Corinth, and Ephesus. He was arrested by the Roman tribune in Jerusalem, and his case was supervised by two corrupt Roman governors at Caesarea before being remanded (as a consequence of Paul's own appeal) to the emperor's tribunal in Rome.

In Paul's letters to Philemon and to the Philippians, second-century readers would also have encountered Paul bound with Roman chains. The image of Paul confined to chains by the Roman authorities is also to be found in Colossians, Ephesians, and 2 Timothy.

In the New Testament it is above all the book of Revelation that transmits messages concerning the past and future martyrdom of the Lamb's followers. Because of his technique of recapitulation, John's reports concerning martyrdom appear intermittently throughout his book. In his own day Christians may have been

subject to harassment by the imperial authorities in ways sh
martyrdom, for example, "licensing," which involved the sign ᴜᵣ
the beast. However, it is particularly for the imprisonment and
martyrdom that are still to come that the Seer prepares the members of his audience (2:10; 6:11b).

STRATEGIES FOR CHRISTIAN DISCIPLES
VIS-À-VIS IMPERIAL ROME

At the same time that the above-mentioned texts alerted Christian
readers to the phenomenon of persecution from the Roman authorities, these texts, plus Paul's Letter to the Romans, provided readers
with counsels and strategies for conducting themselves as Jesus'
disciples in their ongoing dealings with the Roman authorities.

Like later generations of his disciples, Jesus lived under Roman
rule and faced Roman demands for taxation and for compliance
with the established Roman order. How did Jesus himself respond
to these demands? As they pondered the texts of the four Gospels,
second-century Christians would have found that the Gospel of
Luke provided the most substantive answer to this question.
Essentially they would have learned that Jesus' approach was to
evaluate "the things of Caesar" (the programs, policies, and patterns of Roman rule) against the standard of "the things of God"
(the social values and the social patterns desired by God). Luke's
passages concerning service and humility and his passage concerning Roman tribute have primary relevance on this point.

In Jesus' teaching, humility and service were fundamental to the
social conduct that God desired. They were, in effect, the charter
qualities from which to evaluate Roman rule or indeed any type of
sociopolitical order. Was there regard for the poor and the lowly?
Was there a desire to live without recourse to violence? Was there
a sense of God's dominion over all of creation, over every people
and nation? Jesus' words in Luke 22:24–27 clearly expressed reser-
vations about the Roman rulers' fulfillment of the criteria of service and humility.

As it is depicted in the Synoptic accounts, Jesus' approach to
taxation was highly nuanced. In Luke 20:20–26 (cf. Mark 12:13–17;

Matt. 22:15–22), Jesus gave no direct answer as to whether he himself paid the taxes demanded by Rome. Rather his answer implied that the things of Caesar would first have to be evaluated against the standard of the things of God before any judgment about taxation could be given. This reply was just as unsatisfactory from a Roman point of view as it was from a Zealot point of view.

It is also significant that in Luke 13:31–33, Jesus was less than deferential to Herod Antipas, going so far as to disparage him as "that fox." This same highly independent stance is evident also at the trials before Pilate and Herod Antipas. When questioned by Pilate, Jesus was terse and without deference, responding only, "You have said so" (23:3b). When questioned by Herod, he cooperated not at all, refusing to answer Herod's repeated questions (23:9).

To be sure, Luke's Jesus did not espouse the Zealot cause of violent resistance to Roman rule. Nor did he present a detailed blueprint for a social order to replace the social order that Roman military power decreed and enforced. Nevertheless, the Jesus that the Christians of the second century met in Luke's Gospel can scarcely be said to be congenial to Roman rule. Speaking generally, this same assessment may be given regarding the figure of Jesus that these readers would have encountered in the Gospels of Mark and Matthew.

In reading the Gospel of John for guidance regarding their response to Roman rule, second-century Christians would have found less of Jesus' specific teachings and more emphasis on Jesus' unsurpassed sovereignty. Because John's Gospel is written in a different key, it contains negligible counsel regarding the payment of Roman taxes. However, because of his extended account of Jesus' Roman trial, John's readers would have learned Jesus' perspective concerning the circumscribed nature of Roman power. They would also have gained the perspective that Jesus' kingdom was grounded not in violence but rather in witness to the truth.

Because of the guidance it provided in terms of the idolatrous claims advanced by and on behalf of the Roman emperors, John's Gospel would have been especially valued by Christian readers and auditors. They would have found themselves over and over again encouraged to affirm the unsurpassed sovereignty of Jesus. If they actually faced formal trials before imperial governors, John's account could only have inspired them to respond that Jesus was "my Lord and my God" and that Jesus was uniquely "the Savior of the World."

This same concept of giving absolute allegiance to Jesus and to God is also a concept that second-century Christians would have derived from reading the Acts of the Apostles. The principles articulated by Peter, John, and the other apostles when they twice testified before the Sanhedrin would have had continued relevance for later Christians facing comparable situations. Peter and John initially rejected the Sanhedrin's order that they desist from preaching about Jesus. Then, when they were charged with this offense, Peter's response was uncompromising: "We must obey God rather than humans" (5:29). In other words, in the event of a conflict between the things that God desires and the things that the political authorities insist upon, Christians were called to make manifest that their primary allegiance was to God. It was not that the apostles were anti-Roman. It was simply that their fundamental allegiance always belonged to Jesus.

In Paul's case, this radical allegiance was the consequence of his dramatic experience of the sovereign Jesus on the road to Damascus. As a result of his conversion, Paul did not renounce his Roman citizenship or launch a radical critique of Roman domination. However, in a scenario repeated within the narrative many times, Paul became so zealous in proclaiming the sovereign name of Jesus that he was repeatedly arraigned before the Roman authorities of various provinces on the grounds of being a de facto disturber of Roman peace and order.

Given Luke's reports in Acts, it may not be said that Paul ever deliberately strove to engender unrest. Nevertheless, turbulence and upheaval followed in his wake. Very significantly, when Paul was afforded an opportunity to present a defense of his conduct before various provincial authorities, his fundamental explanation centered on the lordship of Jesus. Further, from the time of his arrest in Jerusalem until more than four years later in Rome, Acts portrays Paul as a Roman prisoner in chains. Indeed, Luke ends his work with Paul at center stage, a chained prisoner in Rome, testifying with all boldness that Jesus is Lord.

The conjectured impact of Paul's letters upon later Christians is a topic that must be approached cautiously. Since almost nothing is known of the circulation patterns of Romans, Philemon, and

Philippians, it is hypothetical to posit that all three of these letters were circulating among the various centers of Christian life in the first decades of the second century. Nevertheless, as a mechanism for reviewing this study's findings regarding Paul's "trajectory," let it be assumed that copies of all three letters did circulate widely perhaps as components of a Pauline corpus. Assume also that the second-century Christians who had access to these letters knew that Romans was written before Paul's imprisonment and that Philippians was written from Rome after Paul had experienced a considerable interval as a chained prisoner.

In such a scenario, these readers would have been positioned to grasp that Paul's counsel to the Philippians superseded the counsel that he had earlier expressed in Romans about being subject to the Roman authorities and paying all demanded taxes. They would also have grasped that Paul's definitive perspective, expressed in Philippians, was that it was the Roman authorities themselves who possessed the obligation of being subject to Jesus, of acclaiming him as Lord and genuflecting before him. These same readers would also have realized that the counsel of Philippians superseded that of Titus 3:1, a letter written by, or attributed to, Paul during his pre-imprisonment ministry.

Further, Paul had spoken of the Roman society familiar to him and to the Christians at Philippi as "a crooked and perverse generation" (2:15b). Because they lived as "enemies of the cross of Christ" and "glor[ied] in their shame," the leading figures of this society would ultimately find that "their end is destruction" (3:18–19). In contrast, Christians on earth were to hold fast to the standards of their heavenly citizenship, trusting that they would ultimately be vindicated by Christ, whose power "enables him to subject all things to himself" (3:20–21).

How would second-century Christians have regarded the counsel of 1 Peter and of Revelation? Given that Philippians superseded the counsel of Romans 13:1–7 and Titus 3:1, the two polar positions on the spectrum of New Testament counsels relative to Roman rule are held by 1 Peter and Revelation. (Significantly, both of these documents expressly have Christians in Asia as a part of their intended audiences.) 1 Peter explicitly advocated cooperation with the Roman authorities and explicitly counseled honor for the emperor. In contrast, in Revelation the power of the Roman rulers was of demonic origin and to be resisted on all fronts, albeit not with violent means. In terms of historical perspective, 1 Peter seemed to assume the existence of the empire and its rulers into the foreseeable future. In contrast, Revelation was insistent that imperial Rome merited the judgment of God for the martyrdom of Christians and for its other offenses. As a consequence, in the not distant future, imperial Rome, in all of its power and all of its wealth, would be brought to a catastrophic end.

Summary. It can also be supposed that many who became Christian in the first decades of the second century explicitly expressed a commitment to Jesus as their Lord. Their belief in Jesus as truly Lord and truly Savior could only have been strengthened from their reading and hearing of the texts of John's Gospel, the Acts of the Apostles, and Paul's letters. If they then asked what stance Jesus, *their Lord,* had taken toward the Roman authorities and their empire, they would have found much to ponder in Luke's Gospel and in the other Synoptic accounts.

From these accounts they would have learned to evaluate the Roman policies and practices on the basis of humility and service, on the basis of all of "the things of God." They would also have been alerted to the possibility of testifying before governors and kings, and the possibility of facing a martyr's death. Jesus himself had predicted such developments, and he himself had faced a Roman trial and then death by crucifixion.

Within the framework of this strongly Jesus-oriented approach, they would also have had to ponder the divergent counsels of 1 Peter and Revelation. As they proceeded to evaluate the Roman empire on the basis of Jesus' counsels, would they have concluded with 1 Peter that the Roman governors were sent by the emperor "to punish those who do wrong and praise those who do right" (2:14)? Or would they have concluded with the author of Revelation that Roman rule was essentially demonic, something to resist and withdraw from? The chasm between 1 Peter's assessment and Revelation's assessment of the Roman system must be recognized and even emphasized. Nevertheless, for Christians in the middle or late decades of the second century, this divergence might have been comprehensible.

If there was a significant interval between the dates of composition of 1 Peter and Revelation, and if, during this interval, the Roman authorities significantly altered various imperial policies and practices affecting Christians and others, then the divergence between Revelation and 1 Peter may not have been as startling for second-century Christians as it is for modern readers, who must reckon with the possibility that both documents were authored in close temporal proximity. It is useful to reiterate the hypothesis that is now being proposed. According to the present hypothesis, second-century Christians would have undertaken their own evaluation of Rome's imperial practices knowing that, at one point in time, the author of 1 Peter had counseled full subjection to the imperial authorities. Nevertheless, these Christians would also have known that, at another point in time, the author of Revelation had urged a thoroughgoing resistance to an empire he regarded as demonic.

THE NEW TESTAMENT WRITINGS AND CHRISTIANS IN THE THIRD MILLENNIUM

The preceding section has conjectured regarding the utilization of the New Testament texts by Christians still living under Roman rule in the second century of the first millennium. What can be said regarding the utilization of the New Testament texts by disciples of Jesus living under highly varied political conditions at the beginning of the third millennium?

It is a commonplace to note that, at the time when the New Testament writings first began to circulate, virtually *every* disciple of Jesus lived within the context of Roman rule. At the beginning of the third millennium, the Roman empire is a distant historical reality. Nevertheless, many contemporary Christians face political persecution, and not insignificant numbers are proximate to martyrdom at the hands of contemporary "imperial" authorities. Many other Christians are free from persecution but face challenges in responding to programs, policies, and taxes initiated by governments who reject any explicit reference to the standards of the Gospel. How shall contemporary Christians who face these and other political contexts derive guidance from the writings of the New Testament?

While a comprehensive response to this last question requires recourse to the theological discipline of Christian ethics, it is possible to indicate four principal ways in which the conclusions reached in the preceding chapters have relevance.

1. The first contribution of the present study is its conclusion that Jesus' own approach to Roman rule and to the authorities who administered it was "evaluative." The Jesus who is portrayed in the Synoptic Gospels followed a course that rejected the violence upon which Roman rule was based without thereby embracing the revolutionary violence promoted by the Zealots. In effect, this Jesus maintained that humility, service, and the other values and patterns pertaining to "the things of God" were the fundamental standards against which Roman policies and demands were to be assessed. These standards were to be employed in determining one's response to Roman taxation, and they were to be the basis for evaluating every other imperial practice.

2. The second contribution is to illuminate the way in which the "evaluative" approach of Jesus is a fundamental resource for Christians seeking guidance for their own stance toward contemporary political situations and entities. That the evaluative approach of the Synoptic Jesus is *fundamental* for contemporary Christians is a conclusion that can now be explicitly articulated for the first time. It is a conclusion that emerges from reflection on the findings made in chapters 4, 5, and 7 above.

Speaking generally, John's Gospel, as analyzed in chapter 4 and the Acts of the Apostles as analyzed in chapter 5 both emphasize strongly that Jesus is fully sovereign, and both insist that unqualified allegiance is due to him alone. These emphases on sovereignty and allegiance are highly significant for the potential encouragement they afford contemporary Christians who face the prospect of martyrdom. Nevertheless, in and of themselves, these texts do not explicate the specifics of Jesus' approach to the political order. Readers of the Gospel of John and Acts who do not face the prospect of martyrdom, but rather the ongoing discernment of Christian social conduct, would thus find themselves turning to the Synoptic accounts and especially to Luke's Gospel for detailed information regarding the approach that Jesus adopted and counseled.

Throughout much of Christian history, Romans 13:1–7 has been considered a highly authoritative teaching, if not *the* authoritative teaching for guiding Christians in their approach to the political order. Yet Christians of the third millennium who accept the findings made in chapter 7 above would no longer accord this degree of authority to Romans 13. Christians who are persuaded by the analysis of chapter 7 would now regard Romans 13:1-7 only as Paul's initial counsel on this matter, a counsel that Paul himself implicitly set aside in Philippians.

Further, when they then turned to Philippians, they would achieve insights in two principal areas. First, they would find themselves pondering the various ways in which this letter so memorably testifies to the sovereignty of Jesus. Second, they would be presented with the concept of heavenly citizenship as the standard for assessing earthly conduct, a concept not far from the counsel of "evaluation" advanced by Jesus in the Synoptic Gospels.

3. In delineating that 1 Peter and Revelation rendered two radically divergent judgments regarding the Roman imperial system, the present study may also assist contemporary Christians by alerting them to the complexity that can be involved in the evaluation of political entities, policies, and systems. In given circumstances, contemporary Christians may find themselves evaluating a particular political system and reaching conclusions comparable to those reached by the author of Revelation. Nevertheless, the assessment of other Christians regarding *the same* political policy or system might conceivably be more in the mode of the author of 1 Peter.

In an alternative reconstruction, the situation of Christians in second-century Asia can be appealed to as providing a biblical precedent for startlingly divergent evaluations of the same political reality. In the preceding section of this chapter, it has been suggested that a significant interval of time might have separated 1 Peter and Revelation. The possibility that these two documents were sent to the Christians of Asia at virtually the same time must now be considered. If this were the case, then the Christians who received these two documents would have received seemingly irreconcilable perspectives on the Roman imperial system.

Careful *reflection* would thus be a definite requirement for all Christians undertaking the evaluation of a given political regime. Careful *dialogue* would also be a pressing requirement when contemporary Christians recognize that other members of the Christian community have reached significantly different conclusions about how a particular political entity reflects, or does not reflect, "the things of God." Paul's own inner dialogue, over a period of years, as he assessed and reassessed the Roman imperial system is also instructive for contemporary Christians as they seek to carry out their own respective reflections and dialogues relative to complex political entities and programs.

4. The fourth contribution that the present study affords to contemporary disciples of Jesus is a heightened appreciation for the evocative images and titles that the New Testament writings present regarding Jesus and his response to the political order that surrounded him. Memorable images abound within these texts, and these images serve as powerful resources for contemporary Christians just as they have so served for Christians throughout history. Indeed, one might imagine a meditative book on Christian ethics whose chapter headings would flow from these wonderful images and titles of acclaim.

As a means of bringing this study to a formal conclusion, a partial listing of these images and titles is now provided: (1) Jesus' teaching regarding service and humility; (2) Jesus with the coin of tribute; (3) Jesus arrested and vulnerable before the political authorities; (4) Jesus crucified by Roman soldiers; (5) Jesus, the Lamb who was slain; (6) Jesus, risen Lord; (7) Jesus, Lord and God; (8) Jesus, the Savior of the World. It is an arguable thesis that such images, titles, and teachings constitute the central legacy of the New Testament for contemporary Christians who strive to discern and live faithful discipleship within highly diverse political contexts.

Bibliography

T HIS BIBLIOGRAPHY LISTS WORKS cited in the text as well as other selected works. Readers seeking bibliography for the Gospels, the Acts of the Apostles, and the letters of Paul should consult the following works by R. Cassidy: *Jesus, Politics, and Society: A Study of Luke's Gospel* (Maryknoll, N.Y.: Orbis Books, 1978); "Matthew 17:24–27—A Word on Civil Taxes," *Catholic Biblical Quarterly* 41 (1979): 571–80; *Society and Politics in the Acts of the Apostles* (Maryknoll, N.Y.: Orbis Books, 1983); *John's Gospel in New Perspective: Christology and the Realities of Roman Power* (Maryknoll, N.Y.: Orbis Books, 1992); *Paul in Chains: The Impact of Roman Imprisonment in the Letters of Paul* (New York: Crossroad, 2001). Each of these works also identifies important references in the secondary literature pertaining to Roman rule.

1. Ancient Sources Pertaining to Roman Rule

Augustus to Nero: A Sourcebook on Roman History 31BC—AD 68. Edited by D. Braund. London: Croom Helm, 1985.

The Digest of Justinian. 4 volumes. Latin text edited by T. Mommsen. Translated by A. Watson. Philadelphia: University of Pennsylvania Press, 1985.

Dio Cassius. *Dio's Roman History.* Translated by E. Cary. Loeb Classical Library. Cambridge, Mass.: Harvard University Press, 1914.

Flavius Josephus. *The Jewish Antiquities.* Translated by H. Thackeray and others. Loeb Classical Library. Cambridge, Mass.: Harvard University Press, 1930.

------. *The Jewish War.* Translated by H. Thackeray. Loeb Classical Library. Cambridge, Mass.: Harvard University Press, 1928.

------. *The Life and Against Apion.* Translated by H. Thackeray and others. Loeb Classical Library. Cambridge, Mass.: Harvard University Press, 1926.

Philo. *The Embassy to Gaius.* Translated by F. Colson. Loeb Classical Library. Cambridge, Mass.: Harvard University Press, 1942.

Pliny. *Letters.* Translated by W. Melmoth and W. Hutchinson. Loeb Classical Library. Cambridge, Mass.: Harvard University Press, 1915.

Suetonius. *The Lives of the Caesars.* Translated by J. Rolfe. Loeb Classical Library. Cambridge, Mass.: Harvard University Press, 1913.

Tacitus. *The Annals.* Translated by J. Jackson. Loeb Classical Library. Cambridge, Mass.: Harvard University Press, 1913.

------. *Dialogus. Agricola. Germania.* Translated by W. Peterson. Loeb Classical Library. Cambridge, Mass.: Harvard University Press, 1914.

------. *The Histories.* Translated by C. Moore. Loeb Classical Library. Cambridge, Mass.: Harvard University Press, 1931.

Wallace, S. *Taxation in Egypt from Augustus to Diocletian.* Princeton, N.J.: Princeton University Press, 1938.

2. Studies Pertinent to Christians and Roman Rule

Aland, K. "Das Verhaltnis von Kirche und Staat nach dem Neuen Testament und den Aussagen des 2. Jahrhunderts." In *Neutestamentliche Entwürfe,* edited by K. Aland, 26–123. Munich: Kaiser, 1979.

Barrett, C. K. "The New Testament Doctrine of Church and State." In *New Testament Essays,* 1–19. London: SPCK, 1972.

Cranfield, C. "The Christian's Political Responsibility According to the New Testament." *Scottish Journal of Theology* 15 (1962): 176–92.

Cullmann, O. *The State in the New Testament.* London: SCM, 1957.

Dibelius, M. "Rom und die Christen im ersten Jahrhundert." In M. Dibelius, *Botschaft und Geschichte,* 2:177–228. Tübingen: Mohr, 1956.

Green, B. *Like a Tree Planted: An Exploration of Psalms and Parables Through Metaphor.* Collegeville, Minn.: Liturgical Press, 1997.

Lohmeyer, E. *Christuskult und Kaiserkult.* Tübingen: Mohr, 1919.

Marshall, H. "New Occasions Teach New Duties? 2. The Use of the

New Testament in Christian Ethics." *The Expository Times* 105
(1994): 131–36.

Pilgrim, W. *Uneasy Neighbors: Church and State in the New Testament.* Minneapolis: Fortress, 1999.

Roetzel, C. *Paul: The Man and the Myth.* Minneapolis: Fortress, 1999.

Schrage, W. *Die Christen und der Staat nach dem Neuen Testament.* Gütersloh: Mohn, 1971.

———. *The Ethics of the New Testament.* Translated by D. Green. Philadelphia: Fortress, 1988.

Wengst, K. *Pax Romana and the Peace of Jesus Christ.* Translated by J. Bowden. Philadelphia: Fortress, 1987.

Windisch, H. *Imperium und Evangelium im Neuen Testament.* Kiel: Lipsius & Tischer, 1931.

Wright, N. T. "The New Testament and the 'State.'" *Themelios* 16 (1990): 11–17.

3. Studies Treating 1 Peter

Achtemeier, P. *1 Peter.* Minneapolis: Fortress, 1996.

Best, E. *1 Peter.* London: Oliphants, 1971.

Boismard, M.-É. "Pierre (Première Epître de)." In *Dictionnaire de la Bible,* Supplement, vol. 7, cols. 1415–55. Paris: Letouzey & Ané, 1966.

Elliott, J. *A Home for the Homeless.* Philadelphia: Fortress, 1981.

———. "Disgraced Yet Graced: The Gospel According to Peter in the Key of Honor and Shame." *Biblical Theology Bulletin* 25 (1995): 166–78.

Goppelt, L. *A Commentary on 1 Peter.* Translated by J. Alsup. Grand Rapids: Eerdmans, 1993.

Kelly, J. N. *A Commentary on the Epistles of Peter and Jude.* London: Black, 1969.

McDonald, P. "The View of Suffering Held by the Author of I Peter." Forthcoming in *Suffering, Society, and Scripture,* edited by A. Tambasco. New York: Paulist, 2001.

Talbert, C., ed. *Perspectives on First Peter.* Macon, Ga.: Mercer University Press, 1986.

4. Studies Treating Revelation

Bauckham, R. *The Climax of Prophecy.* Edinburgh: Clark, 1993.

———. *The Theology of the Book of Revelation.* Cambridge: Cambridge University Press, 1993.

Collins, A. Y. *Crisis and Catharsis.* Philadelphia: Westminster, 1984.

Mathews, S. "Salvific Suffering in John's Apocalypse." Forthcoming in *Suffering, Society, and Scripture,* edited by A. Tambasco. New York: Paulist, 2001.

Murphy, F. *Fallen Is Babylon.* Harrisburg, Pa.: Trinity Press International, 1998.

Roloff, J. *Revelation.* Translated by J. Alsup. Minneapolis: Fortress, 1993.

Talbert, C. *The Apocalypse.* Louisville, Ky.: Westminster John Knox, 1994.

Thompson, L. *The Book of Revelation.* New York: Oxford, 1990.

Index of Ancient Sources

Old Testament		9	20–21	22:16	25
Proverbs		9:7–9	31	22:18	25
24:21–22	74	9:48b	21	22:24–25	20
		9:60	25	22:24–27	1, 21, 26, 127
New Testament		11:43	21	22:35–38	24
Matthew		12:22–31	25	22:47–51	24–25
10:17–22	126	13:1–3	20	23:2	20, 24
14:1–12	31	13:9–12	126	23:3	27, 128
17:24–27	32, 33	13:31	26	23:9	27, 128
17:25b–26	33	13:31–33	20, 128		
17:27	33	13:32–33	26	John	
20:24–28	1	14:1–7	21	1:1	37
22:15–22	128	14:11	21	3:17	46
22:21–22	33	14:12–14	22	4	45
25:35–40	32	15:1–2	20	4:42	45
		16:16	25	11:3–4	44
Mark		17:3–4	24	11:21–22	44
6:14–29	31	17:7–10	21	11:23–26	44
10:41–45	1, 31	18:9–14	21	11:27	44
12:13–17	127	19:1–9	22	11:32b	44
		19:1–10	20	11:41b–42	44–45
Luke		19:45–46	20, 23	11:43–44	45
2:1–7	19	20:1–8	23	12:44	46
3:1–2	19	20:9–18	20, 23	13:13–14a	44
3:20	31	20:19	23	14:27	48
4:4–6	105	20:20	23	16	41
4:5–6	35, 36n. 10	20:20–26	20, 27, 127	16:2	41, 126
4:43	25	20:25	28, 73	18:33b	38
5:27–32	20	20:45–47	21	18:34	38
6:15	35	21	26	18:35	38
6:27–28	24	21:12–15	26	18:36	38, 48
6:35–36	25	21:12–19	126	18:37	38
7:34	20	22	20	19:9b	39

19:10	39
19:11	39, 50n. 2
20:13	44
20:28	47
20:30–31	43
21	41
21:15–17	42
21:18	42
21:18–19	41, 126
21:19	42
21:22b	42
21:25	37, 43

Acts
1:13	20, 35
4:19–20	54
4:29	56
4:30	57
5:29	55, 129
5:29–32	54
5:33–42	55
6:15	20
7	54
12	52, 56
12:1–11	56
16	18n. 3, 58
16:20–21	58
17	59
17:6–7	59, 64
18:13	59
19	59
19:21	53
20:13	60
21–24	52
21:11	60
21:23	60
21:33a	60
21:39a	61
22:28	61
22:25–29	66n. 3
22:30	61
23:35b	62
24:23	62
24:24–25	62
24:26	62
24:27	62
25	52
25:9	63
25:9–12	67n. 3
25:10–11	64
25:11	53
25:14–22	63
25:26	64

26:29	63
28	65
28:15	65
28:16b	63
28:20b	63
28:30	65
28:31	66

Romans
13	68, 73, 75, 76, 77, 81n. 4, 90, 134
13:1	76, 91
13:1–7	50n. 2, 68, 70–73, 74, 75, 76, 78, 79, 81n. 4, 82n. 9, 83nn. 10, 12, 84, 86, 87, 90, 95, 101, 102, 130, 134
13:5	76, 91
13:7	83n. 11
13:11b–12a	74
15:19	74
15:19b	69
15:23a	69
15:25–28	87

1 Corinthians
1:23	102n. 3
16:21	97

2 Corinthians
11:23	75

Galatians
5:11	102n. 3

Ephesians
3:1	98
3:13	98
4:1	98
6:18b–20	98

Philippians
1:7b	85
1:13a	85, 86
1:14–18	85, 86
1:20	85
1:27	92
1:27–30	93
2	90
2:6–7	90
2:6–11	90
2:8–11	91

2:15	130
2:15–16	91
2:17	85
2:19–22	86
2:23	85
2:25–30	85
3:2–3	90
3:7–11	93
3:8b–11	94
3:10b	50n. 3
3:17–4:1	91
3:18–19	91, 92, 130
3:20–21	92, 130
3:25–30	90
4:1	92
4:2–3	90
4:22	86

Colossians
1:24	96, 97
4:3	97
4:3–4	96
4:7–14	97
4:10	96
4:18	96

1 Timothy 76–81
1:17	77
2:1–2	77, 83n. 12
6:15	77

2 Timothy
1:8	100
1:10	101
1:11–12	100
1:15	100
1:16–17	100
1:17	95, 99, 100
2:9	100
2:18	100
4:1	101
4:8	95, 99, 101
4:10	100
4:13	95, 99
4:16	95, 99, 100
4:17b–18	101

Titus 76–81
3:1	68, 76, 130

Philemon
1	85, 87
9	85, 87, 88

Philemon (*cont.*)
10   85, 87, 89
13   87
22   86, 88, 89
23   89
23–24   85, 86, 87

Hebrews
10:32–39   126
12:4   126

1 Peter   76–81
1:6   78
2:12   78, 79
2:13–14   68
2:13–17   78, 79, 80,
                  81, 83nn. 10, 13
2:14   131
2:15   78, 79, 80,
                         83n. 12
2:17   80
2:20b   80
2:23   80
2:23–24a   78
3:9   78
3:15–16   78, 82n. 8
3:16   78
3:17–18   80
3:18   78
4:1   78
4:4   78
4:12   78
5:13   78, 81

Revelation
1:1   105
1:3   105
1:5   109
1:9   105
2   119
2:3   119
2:10   106, 118, 127
2:13   107, 119
3   119

3:8b   119
3:10   106
3:12c   119
4   122n. 10
4:1–22:5   105
4:11   108
5:6   120
5:11–13   108–9
5:12   120
6:9–10   111–12
6:9–11   106
6:11b   118, 127
6:12   115
6:15   111
8:13   115
11:8   111
11:13   115
12:9   114
12:12   114
12:13–17   114
13   36n. 10, 110,
                          117, 118
13:1   112
13:2b   114
13:4   105, 113, 114
13:5–6   112
13:6   113
13:10c   117
13:12b–14   113
13:17   118
14   105, 117, 119, 120
14:1b   121
14:8   111, 115, 122n. 7
14:9b–11   119
14:12   117
14:20   115
16   105, 112
16:6   106, 112
16:9   111
16:13   110
16:18   115
16:19   111, 122n. 7
17   105, 112
17:1ff.   111

17:5   111, 122n. 7
17:6   106, 112
17:14   109, 115
17:16   115
17:17   111
18   105, 113, 115
18:2   122n. 7
18:2ff.   111, 115
18:4   117
18:7b   113
18:8   115
18:10   116, 122n. 7
18:13   123n. 15
18:17   116
18:19   117
18:21   115, 122n. 7
18:21–24   116
18:24   106, 112
19   105, 116
19:2   111
19:11–16   109
19:17–21   116–17
19:19–20   115
19:20   110
20:4   106, 121
20:10   115, 116
21:9   115
22:3–5   121
22:7   105
22:18   105
22:19   105

Other Ancient Sources
Josephus
Antiquities
18.1.1   17
Jewish War
2.8.1   16–17

Tacitus
Agricola
30–31   16
Annals
15.44   15

Index of Names and Subjects

Achtemeier, P., 81n. 5,
  82nn. 6, 7, 8, 9,
  83n. 10
Antonius Felix, 35, 52,
  61
apocalyptic literary
  genre, 104–5, 110
Augustus
  rule of, 5–11
  successors of, 11–15
auxiliaries, 7–8, 12
  See also legionaries;
    military; praetorian
    guard

Battle of Actium, 6
Bauckham, R., 121n. 1,
  122n. 10, 123n. 16
Boismard, M.-É., 82nn. 6,
  7
Brutus
  and assassination of
    Julius Caesar, 6

Cassidy, R., 17n. 1, 18nn.
  2, 5, 7, 35n. 1,
  36nn. 5, 8, 9, 50nn.
  1, 4, 66n. 1, 81n. 1,
  102n. 1, 122nn. 8,
  9, 123n. 19
Cassius
  and assassination of
    Julius Caesar, 6

chief priests, 20, 23, 56
  in Acts, 52
Christians
  encouragement of,
    117–21
  persecution of, 14,
    40–42, 111, 125–27
  citizenship, Roman, 10,
    67
Claudius, 12, 13, 52, 73
Colossians, Letter to,
  95–97
course of honors. *See*
  cursus honorum
crucifixion, 42, 102n. 3
  sentence of, 22
cursus honorum (course
  of honors), 10, 22,
  32

Delling, G., 83n. 10
domination model, 19, 30
Domitian, 12, 13, 14, 16,
  46, 49, 107

Elliott, J., 81n. 5
emperors
  and ruler cult, 13, 108
  vulnerability of,
    12–13
Ephesians, Letter to,
  95–99
equestrian class, 12

Felix. *See* Antonius Felix
Festus. *See* Porcius Festus
freedmen, 12

Gaius, 12, 13, 52
Galba, 12, 13
Gamaliel, 55
Gentiles
  Jesus and, 22
Goppelt, L., 82nn. 6, 9,
  83nn. 10, 11, 13
Green, B., 36n. 3

Herod Agrippa I, 52, 56,
  126
Herod Agrippa II, 52, 64
Herod Antipas, 19, 20,
  26–27, 31–32, 128
Herodian dynasty, 10
Herod Philip, 19
Heussi, K., 82n. 6
humility-service model,
  19, 20–25, 36n. 6,
  127
  in Gospel of Mark,
    31–33
  in Gospel of
    Matthew, 32–33

James
  martyrdom of, 52, 56,
    126

Jerusalem community
  political stance of,
    53–57
Jerusalem temple, 20
  destruction of, 107
  Jesus and, 22
Jesus
  accusations against,
    23–24
  and chief priests, 23
  evaluative approach
    of, 133–34
  in Gospel of John,
    37–50
  in Gospel of Mark,
    31–33
  in Gospel of
    Matthew, 31–33
  images and titles of,
    43–46, 135
  kingship of, in John,
    38–39
  Lukan portrayal of,
    19–30
  predictions of, regard-
    ing Roman persecu-
    tion, 40–42
  relationship to
    Roman authorities,
    19, 25–30, 32–33
  sentence of cruci-
    fixion of, 22, 91,
    126
  sovereignty of, 37–40
  as Word, 37
  as Zealot, 23–24
John the evangelist, 43
  perspective of, on
    Roman rule, 43
Josephus, 16–17
Judas Maccabeus, 17
Julius Caesar, 16
  assassination of, 6

Kelly, J. N., 82n. 6; 83n.
    11
kingdom of God, 25

Lazarus, 44–45
legionaries, 7–8, 12
  See also military
Lepidus, 6
Lucius Gallio, 35

Lysias, 61, 63
Lysanias, 19

maiestas (treason),
    13–14, 18n. 5, 73
Mark Antony, 6
Martha and Mary, 44–45
  See also Lazarus
Mary and Martha. *See*
    Martha and Mary
military, Roman, 7–10
  See also auxiliaries;
    legionaries; praeto-
    rian guard
Murphy, F., 122n. 6

Nero, 12, 13, 14, 15, 49,
    67n. 5, 72, 91, 107
  and Christians, 14,
    32, 108
  cult of, 108
  and Paul, 89, 93
Nerva, 12
numerology, 105

Octavian, 6–7
  See also Augustus
Otho, 12, 13

parrhēsia (boldness),
    56–57, 99
Paul
  as chained prisoner,
    61–66, 84–103, 126,
    129, 130
  charges against, 59
  and context of Letter
    to the Romans,
    69–70
  controversies of, in
    Acts, 57–61
  eschatological per-
    spective of, 74
  imprisonment of, 32,
    53, 60–61
  portrait of, in Acts
    and the epistles, 2
  and Roman authori-
    ties, 91–95, 102n. 2,
    129
  Roman citizenship of,
    61, 67n. 3, 129
  in Rome, 63, 65

  and sovereignty of
    Jesus, 91–94
Pauline corpus
  chronology of, 69,
    84–87, 130
Peter
  prediction of martyr-
    dom of, 41–42
Peter, First Letter of,
    78–81
Pharisees
  Jesus' criticism of, 21
Philemon, Letter to,
    85–89
  authorship of, 85
Philippi
  Paul and, 58
Philippians, Letter to,
    85–95
  authorship of, 85
  christological hymn
    in, 90–91
  date of, 2
  location of, 86
Pilgrim, W., 123nn. 14,
    18
Pliny
  and persecution of
    Christians, 48–49
  letter of, to Trajan,
    107
Pontius Pilate, 19, 20,
    23, 27, 30, 35,
    38–40, 128
poor
  care of, 127
  Jesus' teaching on, 22
Porcius Festus, 35, 52,
    53, 62, 64
praetorian guard, 7–8, 12,
    13, 89
  See also auxiliaries;
    legionaries; mili-
    tary
prayer
  Jesus and, 25
priesthood
  of Jerusalem temple,
    20
princeps
  office of, 6
prophetic literary genre,
    104–5, 110

recapitulation, 105, 110,
115, 126–27
Revelation, book of,
104–23
authorship of, 105
blasphemy in, 112
date of, 107
idolatry in, 112–13
indictment of Rome
in, 109–14
the Lamb in, 108–9,
120, 123n. 20
literary characteris-
tics of, 104–8
martyrdom in, 106,
111–12
persecution in, 106
political context of,
106
prophecy of Rome's
demise in, 114–17
recapitulation in,
105–6, 110, 115,
126–27
sovereignty of God in,
108–9
Roetzel, C., 67n. 3
Roloff, J., 122nn. 3, 7,
123n. 20
Roman empire
in Acts, 51–66
and Augustus, 5–11
citizenship in, 61, 92
economic exploita-
tion in, 6, 113
infrastructure of, 9
Johannine perspective
on, 2
Lukan perspective on,
2
military in, 7–8
negative portrayal of,
15–17
Pauline perspective
on, 2
and persecution of
Christians, 40–42,
48–50, 125–27

population of, 6
propaganda in, 11
prophecy of demise
of, 114–18
slavery in, 6
taxes in, 8–9, 20,
25–30, 127
trade in, 7
Romans, Letter to the
context of, 69–70
eschatological per-
spective of, 74
instructions in, 70–73
and Roman authori-
ties, 84, 90
Rome
called Babylon, 107,
111, 122n. 7
images of, 111, 123n.
14

Samaritans
Jesus and, 22, 45–46
Sanhedrin, 10, 27
in Acts, 52
authority of, 54–55
in Gospel of John, 41
and martyrdom of
Stephen, 54, 56
and Peter, 54
Satan
and Roman empire,
105
scribes
Jesus' criticism of, 21
senate, Roman, 6–7, 11
Sergius Paulus, 35
sinners
Jesus and, 22
slavery
absence of, in
Judaism, 18
in Roman empire, 6,
123n. 15
Stegemann, W., 67n. 3
Stephen
martyrdom of, 54
symbolism, 105

synagogue authorities,
41

Tacitus, 14–15, 16, 18n.
6, 107
Talbert, C., 82n. 7,
122nn. 2, 11, 123n.
13
tax collectors
Jesus and, 20, 22
Roman, 9
taxes
Jesus and, 20, 25–30,
31–33, 127–28
Paul and, 70–76
Roman, 8–9, 20,
25–30, 127
Thomas
and appearance of
Jesus, 46–48
Tiberius, 11, 12, 13, 19,
73
Timothy, First Letter to
on Roman authori-
ties, 76–77
Timothy, Second Letter
to, 95, 99–101
Titus, 12, 13
Titus, Letter to
on Roman authori-
ties, 76–77
Trajan, 12, 41, 48–49

Vespasian, 12, 13
violence
Jesus' teaching on,
24–25
Vitellius, 12, 13

Wallace, S., 18n. 4
wisdom tradition, Jewish
influence of, on Paul,
74
women
Jesus and, 22

Zealots, 16–17, 74, 95
Jesus and, 20, 23, 33,
128, 133